# Tackling A Level Pr[o] in Computer Scienc[e]

## AQA A Level Computer Science 7517

**Published by**
PG Online Limited
The Old Coach House
35 Main Road
Tolpuddle
Dorset
DT2 7EW
United Kingdom
sales@pgonline.co.uk
www.pgonline.co.uk
**2020**

PG ONLINE

# Preface

This guide to Tackling A Level Projects in Computer Science is designed to give you clear and focused advice to help you maximise your potential when completing your project.

It will take you through all aspects of the project, from document setup, to each stage of the process. This guide will give you tips, and clearly written support to:

- Help you create a professional-looking report
- Outline what is required for each section of the documentation
- Help you to understand the exam board's requirements
- Give advice on how to meet these requirements
- Give you a checklist to help ensure you have completed all required parts of the project

Whilst this guide can be used to support any programming project, it is tailored to meet the requirements and expectations for the AQA A Level Computer Science (7517). It is therefore recommended that this guide is used alongside the specification you are following, in addition to support from your Computer Science teacher.

You should make sure that the project you are proposing is complex enough to meet the requirements of A Level. Your teacher should be able to support you in checking whether your proposed project meets any complexity expectations.

## Acknowledgements

Every effort has been made to trace and acknowledge ownership of copyright. The publishers will be happy to make any future amendments with copyright owners. The author and publisher would like to thank the following companies and individuals who granted permission for the use of their images in this textbook.

Chapter 2 Word screenshots © Microsoft®

Chapter 3 Survey Monkey image: Sharaf Maksumov © / Shutterstock.com

All other images © Shutterstock

First edition 2020
A catalogue entry for this book is available from the British Library
ISBN: 978-1-910523-20-9
Copyright © PG Online 2020
Edited by James Franklin

Printed on FSC® certified paper

Printed and bound in Great Britain by Bell & Bain Limited

# Contents

# Chapter 4 – Documented design                    38

# Chapter 5 – Technical solution                    62

# Chapter 6 – Testing                                69

# Chapter 7 – Evaluation 76

# Chapter 8 – Final checks 82

# Index 87

# Appendix 90

# Chapter 1
## Starting a new project

## Objectives

- Choose a project title
- Choose a stakeholder
- Create a project outline
- Understand levels of technical skills
- Also, understand:
  - How to be realistic in your project scope
  - Languages that are and are not appropriate to use
  - The design methodologies that could be used
  - Different options for IDEs
  - How your work is authenticated

## Introduction

Choosing a suitable A Level project is quite a challenge. Projects contribute to 20% of your final grade and therefore choosing the right project for you is important. In particular, for AQA, you must consider how much opportunity the project you choose gives for demonstrating your technical skills.

This guide will take you through the steps to create a successful project. It will not give you the answers, but instead show you tips and tools to help keep you on track, and evidence your project efficiently. Using this guide and the specification should give you confidence in being able to produce the best project you can.

Projects are not about quantity, but quality. Exam Boards have specific **mark schemes**. You need to show you meet each of the mark scheme points. Clear and precise documentation makes it easier for both you, your teacher and the moderator to identify where you have met **mark criteria**.

| TIP | Ensure that you fully understand the mark scheme before starting your project. |
|-----|--------------------------------------------------------------------------------|

# Chapter 1

## Starting a new project

The most important advice that can be given when undertaking AQA projects is:

1. Most of the marks are given for the technical solution that you program. As such, it is crucial that you spend time at the start of your project choosing an appropriate problem to solve that will give you the opportunity to demonstrate complex technical skills.

2. You may be tempted to spend all the time programming and ignoring the documentation. However, your program is *part* of the project, not all of it.

3. Make sure you choose a project that is realistic, and one that you are capable of completing. If you are motivated to complete the project and find it interesting, then you will be more motivated to overcome the challenges that *will* present themselves.

4. Every section of the project depends on the Analysis. The Analysis is the first part of your project. It is worth spending time making sure this section is done as well as possible. Moving on too quickly may mean that you struggle to complete the Documented design, Technical solution and Testing sections.

> **TIP** Many marks are given to your report. It is important that you work on this throughout your project.

# Choosing a project title

A suitable A Level project requires you to think about:

- Your own confidence levels in programming
- The difficulty of the techniques a solution will require
- Project scope
- End-users
- Languages
- Design strategies
- Time frames
- Exam board requirements

There are almost no restrictions on the types of project which are allowed. All of the following could make good A Level projects:

- Games
- Mapping or route-finding applications
- Automation
- Use of Raspberry Pi or Arduino technology
- Data set analysis
- Using APIs to collate and analyse real-time data
- Mobile phone or tablet apps
- Dynamically generated websites with database backends
- Membership systems
- Scheduling or timetabling systems

The important focus should be on programming in a high-level text-based programming language. Your project must allow you to demonstrate your programming abilities, not just design a graphically appealing website, or use a database that is built with a graphical user interface such as Microsoft® Access®.

> **WARNING** Your project problem and solution must allow enough scope to access the more advanced technical techniques (see more on this in the following section). You should discuss this carefully with your teacher.

# Problems and investigations

Whilst it is up to you what you decide to do as a project, you can ask for help from your teacher when making your decision.

The first choice you have to make is whether you would like to create a solution to a problem or carry out an investigation. The vast majority of students doing AQA projects tackle problems rather than investigations.

## Problems

Most students will find a problem that exists for a group of users or one end-user. Their project then requires analysing and developing a computational solution to the problem.

> **TIP** You will need input from an end-user or other interested people when doing your project.

## Investigations

Instead of a problem, AQA allows you to undertake an investigation of an area of interest that requires a significant amount of programming.

In order to carry out an investigation, you must have a supervisor who has some understanding of the area that will be investigated.

> **TIP** You must have a supervisor in order to carry out an investigation. Your supervisor should not be the teacher who will mark your project.

Examples of investigation projects include:

- AI or machine learning algorithms
- Data set analysis and visualisation – e.g. from live data feeds or large data sets
- Neural networks
- 3D graphics rendering

# Generating project ideas

The first step to a good project is generating good ideas. Your best idea may not be the first one you have. Take time to create a range of ideas.

> **TIP** Always take time to generate as many ideas as possible. Investigate the best ones, and then choose your project.

Generating many ideas may seem hard. However, almost anything can be made into a good project with some thought.

Try this process to create project ideas:

1. Write down a list of all the areas and interests that you have – try to produce at least 10
2. For each of these areas, write down potential problems you think you can solve
   a. Write down **everything** that you think of – you can review them later
   b. Spend at least 30 minutes doing this
   c. Aim to get 20-30 ideas
3. Come back a day later and check - add anything else you think of
4. Wait two days and then pick your favourite 10
5. Narrow these 10 ideas down to five. Try to use your teacher or friends to help
6. Take each of these five ideas and write a small project brief for each
   a. This should be three paragraphs or around 100 words
   b. Narrow down and develop the ideas further
   c. Try to add three main success criteria for each idea
7. Narrow the list down to just three ideas and turn each of them into a longer project proposal
8. Consider carefully how any solution could allow access to more complex technical skills
9. Discuss the proposals with your teacher
   a. Check they have the potential to meet the requirements of the mark scheme
   b. Check they are realistic timewise
   c. Check you will have the resources to do each project
   d. Check they allow you to access the more challenging technical skills that are appropriate for your ability
   e. It may be that your teacher can ask the exam board for advice at this stage if needed
10. Finally, choose the one idea you will take forward for your final project

> **TIP** A variety of A level projects that can be used for ideas can be found on a YouTube channel. See: **www.pgonline.co.uk/landing/a-level-cs-projects**

TASK   Go through the idea generation steps.

# Technical skills

When your project is marked, the types of technical skills that you have used in implementing it will be taken into account.

It is crucial that you consider this carefully before you commit to a particular project as certain problems may not have enough scope to access higher marks.

The different groups for technical skills are given in the AQA project mark scheme. You should make sure that you have a print out of these and familiarise yourself with the expected standard. Projects of an A level standard will typically have designs and implement solutions that involve Group A skills.

Once you have a chosen problem that you would like to solve in your project, discuss this closely with your teacher to see that they agree there is enough scope for you to access the top marks. If you find the subject or programming very difficult, then you may wish to discuss ways that you could solve the problem with Group C skills, but then alter it or add to it with more advanced skills as you gain in confidence.

TIP   You will also be able to demonstrate your technical skills in the quality of programming code you produce. For more about this, see coding styles in Chapter 5.

# Chapter 1
## Starting a new project

## Example of technical skills

The following table illustrates how different levels of skill can be applied to different example problems and solutions.

| Example problem and solution | Technical skills group | Why? |
|---|---|---|
| The project involves the creation of a quiz for students learning about the periodic table of elements. Details about each element are stored in an array and a linear search is used to find particular elements. | C | The project uses a **linear search** (Group C) to find elements. A **single-dimensional** array (Group C) to store information about each element. |
| A simple website is built using a server-side scripting language (such as PHP). The aim of the website is to make it easy for a business owner to monitor certain Twitter keywords. The program uses the Twitter API which responds in JSON format. | B | **Server-side scripting** is being used to **respond to requests** from the user with a **simple client-server model** (Group B). The **Twitter API** is being accessed using **JSON** (Group B). |
| A charity has five minibuses that collect elderly people every day to take them from their home to the shops. The solution allows the users to use a website to enter a day when they would like to be picked up. It then calculates the most efficient route (shortest-path) for the mini-bus and also schedules buses and sends an email to users letting them know when they will be picked up. | A | The solution makes use of Graph **Traversal** (Group A) to find the shortest path. It uses a **complex algorithm** to determine the **scheduling** of each person using the mini-bus and which mini-bus should be used (Group A). **Queue operations** are used to store the order in which each pick-up will be made (Group A). It uses **server-side scripting for a complex client-server model** (Group A) to take requests, perform scheduling and send out emails. |

> **TIP**
> If the algorithms or methods of solving a problem are not given in the table of example technical skills given by AQA, discuss these with your teacher. They may need to ask an AQA adviser for help in determining which group the skills belong to.

# High-achieving project title examples

The following ideas are examples of project ideas that have enough depth to make use of technical skills in Group A.

| Project Title | Brief idea | Potential Group A algorithms and models |
|---|---|---|
| **Revision Quiz** | • Support candidates with revision<br>• Log in and recording system<br>• Database of questions linked to specification/exams<br>• Self-adapting learning algorithms to modify quiz, based on user answers<br>• Predictive charts to show progress and potential grades<br>• Auto-generation of revision plans based on progress | • Complex data model in a database<br>• Cross-table parameterised SQL<br>• Aggregate SQL functions<br>• Complex user-defined algorithms<br>• Complex user-defined use of object-orientated programming (OOP) |
| **Robot Navigation** | • Create a learning algorithm to navigate a maze<br>• Allow the robot to navigate a maze<br>• Show that it learns, as each navigation should be faster<br>• Allow it to deal with random obstacles | • Complex user-defined algorithms<br>• Recursive algorithms<br>• Graph/Tree traversal<br>• Complex robotics model |
| **Twitter Crawler** | • Scrape keywords from a user's Twitter feed<br>• Build a profile of the user's interests<br>• Search for other Twitter feeds with similar interests<br>• Recommend feeds for the user to follow<br>• Adapt based on the user's uptake of these suggestions | • Complex client-server model<br>• Server-side scripting<br>• Calling parameterised Web service APIs and parsing JSON/XML to service a complex client-server model<br>• Complex user-defined algorithms<br>• Complex data model in a database |

| Website data analysis (Investigation) | • Analyse large data sets for web site users to find trends and relationships<br>• Visualise the data | • Complex user-defined algorithms for pattern matching<br>• Graph/Tree traversal<br>• Complex mathematical model<br>• Complex data model in a database<br>• Aggregate SQL functions<br>• User/CASE-generated DDL script |

*Examples of good project titles and ideas*

## Low-achieving project title examples

The following table shows ideas that are likely to result in Group C technical skills being used.

| Project Title | Brief idea | Potential Group C algorithms and models |
|---|---|---|
| Grade calculator | • A teacher adds grades for students<br>• Averages are calculated<br>• Grades are generated | • Single-dimensional arrays<br>• Linear search<br>• Simple mathematical calculations<br>• Non-SQL table access |
| Stock system | • Record incoming stock<br>• Allow sellers to update the stock level<br>• Say when stock items have run out<br>• Print a stock list<br>• Allow new stock items to be added | • Single table database<br>• Simple mathematical calculations |
| Games Quiz | • Has a bank of questions<br>• Asks questions at random<br>• Allows user to select a topic<br>• Records player scores<br>• Prints out best topic answers | • Single table database<br>• Simple mathematical calculations<br>• Single-dimensional arrays |
| Website | • Company static website uses a template for the style of each page<br>• The content is stored in a database | • Single table database |

*Examples of low-achieving project titles and ideas*

Each of these projects currently lack the depth required to access the technical skills of Group A or B. As such, they limit the marks that are available. However, each of the briefs could be adapted to add more depth and give more opportunity. For example, contrast the games quiz with the revision quiz in the first table.

Building websites with database back ends are fine, but the idea should be to use more complex algorithms to process the data in better ways. Projects require programming in a **high-level language**. HTML and CSS will not meet this requirement. Using a server-side language to process data and requests, JavaScript for client-side processing and complex databases with interlinked tables and SQL will help in accessing Group A marks.

Before any final decision is made, check again with your teacher that your project will allow you to access the marks you need for the technical skills.

> **TIP**
> If you are unsure about your project idea and which technical skills group it fits in, it may be possible to send it to AQA to get feedback on it. Ask your teacher about this.

## Projects of an A level standard

Your project should make use of concepts and programming above those covered at GCSE level. All the techniques that are Group C skills are GCSE level. As such, all the low-achieving project ideas above are not of A level standard. As such, these projects would lose a significant number of marks for both the implementation and also the other sections of the report.

By contrast, all the high-achieving project ideas are of an A level standard. They would allow full access to the marks for both the report and implementation.

> **WARNING**
> Your project should have the potential to include algorithms and skills from Group A to solve it. This will ensure that your project is of A level standard.

## Choosing users and people for feedback

When carrying out your Analysis section, you will need to have potential users who can give you feedback. You can choose to have one end-user or multiple users. Other stakeholders who may have an interest in the project may also be used. The person you choose should be a third party and not yourself.

For instance, if the problem is to produce a teaching tool for an area of A-level Maths, it may be that a Maths teacher could act as the key intended end-user. In addition to this, some students may also be involved in the Analysis stage, using an interview or other techniques. As they will also be experiencing the software that is to be created, their views and ideas would be useful to research.

Your intended users do not need to be named. You may, for example, want to develop a computer game. In this case, you may choose to use friends for feedback of different ideas in the Analysis, whilst a teacher or family member may be chosen for more critical feedback in the Evaluation section.

# Chapter 1
## Starting a new project

TIP — You need to have a person or number of people to discuss your requirements within the Analysis section and give feedback in the Evaluation section.

In an investigative project, your supervisor should be able to give the necessary dialogue and feedback for the Analysis and Evaluation sections.

TIP — Successful projects will often have other people involved to help provide ideas and feedback.

Anyone can become involved in your project, but it is better to be careful who you choose. Try to avoid choosing your Computer Science teacher. However, another member of staff could work well as an end-user. For instance, if you are thinking of a fitness tracker app then a member of staff in the PE department could make a good choice.

Choosing classmates or friends may seem like a good idea. However, if you do, you must be sure that they are willing and able to be critical of your system. When it comes to giving feedback on your solution or investigation you want your users or supervisor to provide sensible and **critical feedback**, rather than simply stating that "it all works wonderfully".

The users must have the time to give to your project. They may say yes at first, but will they still be happy to help six months later. Let them know how much time will be required of them, and when. For instance, if you use a teacher, remember that many teachers have coursework or mock exams to mark which may be around the time that you want them to start giving feedback on your solution. This could affect your progress.

If you are only using one user or supervisor, have an alternative person as a backup. This way, if the initial person you are working with cannot help you to the end of your project, then your backup one will be able to step in. It won't be ideal, but it will be better than being left without a user.

TIP — Ensure that the chosen user(s) (or recipients if you are doing an investigation) are suitable, available and willing to give you their time.

Use the following table to see the benefits and drawbacks of using certain types of people as your stakeholder.

| Stakeholder | Benefits | Drawbacks |
|---|---|---|
| Friends | • Generally good availability<br>• Supportive | • Biased towards your project or you<br>• May not have the experience you need<br>• May be unwilling to criticise |
| Teachers | • Experienced in what you need<br>• Impartial | • Can get very busy<br>• May have multiple people asking them<br>• Can have periods where they cannot help due to marking or similar |
| Family | • Likely to be available<br>• Reliable | • Could be biased<br>• May not have experience in the area of your project<br>• May not be able to provide other ideas as solutions |
| Clients | • Know what they want<br>• Able to be critical<br>• Knowledge of the area they work in<br>• Interest in the end product being functional | • May have periods when not available<br>• May not be there for the lifetime of the project<br>• May not be IT experts and demand more than is realistic<br>• May ask for more as the project goes on |
| Users of online communities – e.g. users of forums or IRC channels | • May have an in-depth knowledge of the subject you are studying<br>• May be international experts<br>• Real-world support<br>• Easy to communicate with | • May decide not to respond without notice<br>• May set challenges and expectations that are beyond those of A level<br>• May not be contactable to review your final solution/investigation |

# Choosing a supervisor

If you choose to do an investigation then you will need to choose a supervisor. Your supervisor should be someone other than the teacher who will mark your project. They do not need to be experienced in Computer Science or programming, but they do need to have a good knowledge of the area that you are looking to investigate. For example, an investigation into the auto-generation of artistic landscapes may use an art teacher as a supervisor.

Ideally, a supervisor would be someone external to the school. Examples of good supervisors include:

- People who are professionally employed in the area which your investigation will be studying
- Academics, such as university lecturers, college or school teachers who teach this area as a specialist
- People who have qualifications or programming experience in the area you wish to investigate

> **TIP**
>
> If you are highly motivated to carry out an investigation but cannot find an appropriate supervisor, then if your teacher is willing to act as your supervisor they may be allowed to. Ask them to contact their AQA advisor to see if this would be possible.

# Being realistic

Very large projects may be unrealistic to achieve in the time you have. Often, picking projects which are too ambitious can lead to a mid-project collapse. If your project appears to be becoming too big, a good strategy is to define the core components of the system. Once you have defined these, then ask "What can I add on if I have time?". Thinking this way will remove some of the pressure and make the project more manageable.

For example, a project that tried to create an entire school Management Information System (MIS) would be far too large. This would need a team of programmers to achieve. Instead, choose one aspect of the system that is more achievable such as a timetabling or a complex calendar system that flags up event clashes.

> **TIP**
>
> It is better to do a smaller realistic project well than a more ambitious project badly. Remember that marks are given for the completeness of your solution. These are far easier to achieve for a smaller project.

Big projects will require significantly more testing and implementation time. The designs will be more complex and the write up will become longer. Focus on smaller projects which allow demonstration of the requirements set by AQA and the more advanced technical skills of Group A. Repeating the same technical skills many times may not gain you any extra marks but will increase the amount of work you have to do.

You do not need to show evidence of testing as your solution or programs develop – instead you can test everything at the end once you have finished. That said, if you wish to record unit tests on sections of your program as you produce them then this is allowed and you do not need to repeat the tests later.

Consider using video evidence for some testing. Video testing works especially well on tests for transitions, games and end-user interaction. Free screen capture software is available to help with this - see **www.pgonline.co.uk/landing/a-level-cs-projects** for more information.

You should also plan where you will focus your time and effort. Check how many marks each section is worth in the mark scheme, then ensure that you give yourself enough time to complete each section well. Whilst more than half the marks are given to your programmed solution, don't ignore the importance of your report in evidencing your project and gaining the remainder of the marks.

Larger projects need more drive and focus. Think about how you react to being under pressure when things are not going well. Focus on projects that can be broken down into smaller parts and then merged.

It is advisable to keep a simple project plan with milestones. This will allow you to see early in the project if you are getting behind and then take appropriate actions such as changing the requirements of the project to something more manageable or devoting more time to the project.

> **TIP** Plan your project carefully. Build-in some contingency time for unforeseen problems, then stick to your plan.

> **WARNING** If you intend to remove any requirements once you have started your project, discuss this with your teacher. It is important that your project does not fall below that the expectations required for A-level standard.

# Appropriate difficulty

Choosing a project is a challenging task and depends on a range of aspects.

## How confident are you at programming?

Think about your programming skill level. It is good to learn new things but consider how much time is available. If you cannot learn how to do a new skill, how will this affect the project?

If you are new to programming or find it difficult, you may want to focus on a smaller project which allows you to build the skills needed as well as meet the mark scheme criteria.

Systems that have no online capabilities and work on a local standalone machine are usually a good start. Trying to interface with APIs or multi-user access systems may be too much to begin with.

For example, a simple player vs. computer game can give plenty of opportunities to show skills, and yet keep the concept quite simple.

## What language are you using?

Using many languages may allow you to create a more complex project. However, it is also increasing the risk of failure and challenge within the project. Similarly, choosing to do a project in a language you have never used before will give you far more work to do and be riskier. Sometimes, using what you already know is the best approach.

# Chapter 1

**Starting a new project**

## Exam board requirements

Some decisions may limit the difficulty of technical skills required. You should ideally aim to use technical skills that are in Group A. If your Analysis section only plans for skills that are of Group C standard, then your project will not be of an A Level standard and you will be marked down heavily for all sections of the project.

By contrast, if your project is of an A Level standard and uses technical skills in Group A, then you will be able to access all marks on the mark scheme.

## Thinking modularly

It is a good idea to split your project into modules. Start with a core, which will allow you to demonstrate a good level of programming and skills. Then have 'modules' that you can add to the project to help develop either its challenge or function. Working this way allows milestones to be met. Your project can steadily be built up whilst meeting all sections of the mark scheme well.

# Languages

There are many **languages** that can be used for a project. Some languages suit certain types of project more than others.

The majority of projects will be done in a high-level text-based language. Python, C#, Java, VB.NET and PHP are suitable languages that are commonly used. If databases are used, then SQL is usually used to query them. The exam board generally restricts you from using 'drag and drop' languages, such as GameMaker and Scratch. Any IDE or language that allows you to pre-generate a lot of code is generally not allowed.

> **TIP**
>
> AQA does not restrict the high-level programming language(s) that can be used. Check any languages you are considering using with your teacher. They will need to be confident that they can mark your work.

# Project development

The documentation that you need to write will be very similar whether you have chosen to solve a problem or carry out an investigation.

Your project report should follow five sections:
- Analysis
- Documented design
- Technical solution
- Testing
- Evaluation

However, this doesn't mean that the project needs to be carried out using a traditional systems life cycle. You may use an iterative approach.

## Iterative/Agile

**Iterative** or **Agile** development methodologies are more likely to be used at A Level. This methodology uses short focused cycles. For instance, you may do an iteration on a key algorithm such as an AI feature then do an iteration on the user interface that will control it.

The project will be broken down into sections – each one taking one, or many iterations. By its nature, iterative design is more flexible and it may be easier to alter ideas and change direction.

Iterative design still requires a clear idea of the end product. However, it deals better with unpredictable requirements, or when the final product is initially hard to define. It also allows for more regular user feedback.

Prototypes or early iterations can be produced quickly and then altered as the project develops.

| TIP | Evidence of each iteration taking place does not need to be collected. |
|---|---|

# Choosing an Integrated Development Environment

The **Integrated Development Environment (IDE)** is the software in which you will enter and run your source code. Simple IDEs are often used at GCSE, for example, you may have used IDLE at GCSE for Python programming.

A Level projects will require a significant programming element and choosing an IDE that will provide the support you need is worthwhile.

*MS Visual Studio has many more in-built features to support you more than a simple IDE such as IDLE*

# Chapter 1

## Starting a new project

Many IDEs contain the ability to create file structures, in-program help and support, links to developer communities and so on. Your IDE can either be a great support or add an extra level of challenge.

> **TIP** Some IDEs, such as Visual Studio provide the facility to easily create Graphical User Interfaces (GUIs). Choosing such an IDE early in your project may save you significant amounts of time later.

The options you have for your IDE may be dependent on the programming language that you choose to use.

There are specific environments available for game making such as Unreal Engine or Unity. Other types of project, such as a mobile app or web development will have specific IDEs that help with the implementation of solutions.

# Authentication of work

You need to make sure that the problem you choose to solve or investigate is different from other students in your class. This is to prevent there being any chance of you or a classmate helping or informing each other of ways to solve a problem.

Before you submit your project for assessment, you will need to sign a Candidate Record Form. This states that the work you are submitting is your own work (except for anything that you have declared on the form or acknowledged in the references in your report). Your teacher will also need to sign that the work was produced solely by you.

> **TIP** Before committing to a project title, check that no one else in your class is doing a similar project. Let your classmates know what your project title is so that they do not inadvertently choose something similar.

## To do list
Have you done the following?

☐ Chosen a project title

☐ Created a proposal for your project

☐ Checked with your teacher that your project has enough scope to gain all marks for technical programming skills

☐ Checked with your teacher that your project is of an A level standard to prevent being marked down in the report writing

☐ Considered if the difficulty and size of your proposed project is achievable

☐ Chosen your user(s) if solving a problem OR chosen a supervisor if undertaking an investigation

☐ Checked that no other students in your class are doing a similar project and let them know what project you are doing so they don't do something similar

☐ Chosen the programming language(s) you will use

☐ Chosen the IDE you will use

☐ Got approval on your proposal from your teacher

☐ Created a simple project plan with milestones

# Chapter 2
## The report

## Objectives

- Set up a template for your work
- Create your own headers, footers and styles
- Ensure essential information is shown on your document
- Understand and use referencing correctly

## Setting up the document

When writing a report, there are requirements for what should be included in your report.

Key details need to be included on each page such as your **name**, **candidate number**, **centre number**, **qualification code** and **page number**. If the report is printed for any reason, this will help to identify it and ensure it is in the correct order.

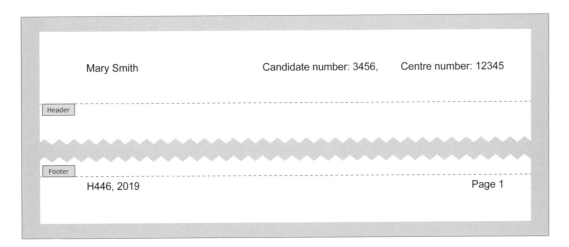

## Word processing software

The best way to create the report is with word processing software. Using presentation software or other software packages is usually not appropriate. Learning how to use a word processing package effectively is key. It will also be a life-long skill.

Word processors have many tools to help you create neatly laid out documents. A well laid out document will be easier for your teacher to mark. It will also make it easier for the moderator to find evidence quickly when checking the marks awarded by your teacher.

Some key features of word processing software that you will find useful in your project:

- Styles which can be used to auto-generate a contents page
- Headers and footers for your candidate details and page numbers
- Page and section breaks
- Tables, borders and shading
- Auto-referencing

# Title page

Your title page should be functional. It does not need to be particularly fancy.

Title pages should have the following information:

- Full name
- Candidate number
- Centre name
- Centre number
- Project title
- Qualification code
- Date

There is no need to have more information than this.

> **TIP** The cover page does not get you extra credit, so do not spend long on creating it.

Many word processing packages have pre-designed cover page templates and styles to use. It is worth looking to see if you like one. This will save you time creating your own.

# Chapter 2
## The report

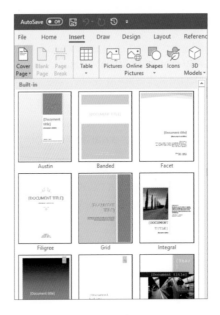

*Selection of Microsoft® Word templates*

| TASK | Create a title page for your documentation. |

# Using styles

**Styles** are pre-set ways of formatting text. You should create and save any styles that are needed before adding any content to your document.

Using styles is important as they will be used later to create a table of contents for your work that will dynamically change as you add or delete pages. This will save you a lot of time.

*Style options within a word processor*

The most common ones you will need are Normal, Heading 1 and Heading 2. Again, there are no extra marks for creating styles. Use the default ones that your word processor or template provide.

You may find that there are certain situations where you need to create your own style. This will be most likely when you wish to add programming code to your report.

When setting up a style for code, remember that it is easiest to read if a monospace font is used. Copying and pasting code from the IDE that you use may also keep the syntax highlighting. This will make it easier for your teacher and moderator to read the code.

Use just one font for your report. This will make your report look more professional. To emphasise text or titles make use of font size, bold or italics. Naturally, computer code may be in a different monospace font.

> **TIP** Your styles should be clean and easy to read. The defaults that come with your word processor should be sufficient, so don't waste time creating your own styles other than for computer code.

Your key sections of the report will have Heading 1 applied to them. The key sections are:

- Analysis
- Documented design
- Technical solution
- Testing
- Evaluation

You should also add sections at the end for References and an Appendix for your program listings.

> **TASK** Define styles for your document.

## Table of contents

A **table of contents** is essential for your documentation. It helps to show the teacher and moderator where your evidence is. Your teacher will use this to help reference their marking on the form that is sent to the exam board.

If you keep your work organised, a table of contents will also help you to refer back to tests, stakeholder success criteria and other parts of your report that you need to reference.

Most word processors will automatically create a table of contents. They make use of styles to produce these. It is essential that you are using styles throughout your report for this to work. Once set up, the table of contents and page numbers can be updated with just one click.

# Chapter 2
## The report

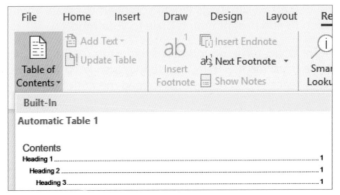

*Word processors insert contents tables automatically if styles have been used correctly*

**TIP** Keep your table of contents and page numbers up to date. It is worth updating the table of contents every time you close the document after working on it.

**TASK** Insert a table of contents after your cover page. Make sure it has automatically generated entries for the key sections you added in the previous task.

# Headers and footers

**Headers and footers** are repeated at the top and the bottom of each page in the report. They should contain the following items:

- Candidate name
- Centre name
- Project title

- Candidate number
- Centre number
- Page number

It is also possible to set up different headers and footers for different sections.

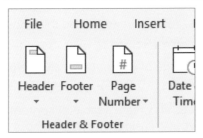

Using different section headers can be useful but they are not needed. If you understand section breaks then it may be worth using them. Otherwise, keep it simple

**TASK** Set up the header and footer for your document.

## Page numbers

**Page numbers** can be inserted automatically. Each page should be numbered. This is good practice and helps later when referencing evidence. They also help your teacher and moderator to find where evidence is located in the report. Positioning page numbers in the bottom right of the report is usually best.

Start the title page as page one. This will make the page numbers of the final PDF version of your report match the page numbers in Word. This will help your teacher and the moderator to navigate the report and any page references within it.

TASK    Ensure that your footer has page numbers in it.

# Referencing

Usually, you will have unlimited access to resources. Therefore, it is important to **reference** any third party resources that are used for support within your project.

Using third party sources (e.g. ideas for code and technical support) is acceptable. Any use of sources **must** be referenced. You must also then show how they have been adapted for your project. This will allow your teacher to give you credit for how you modified the work from your source.

There are two ways to reference. The first is to put a superscript number next to the referenced work and then explain where it came from at the bottom of the page using footnotes.

The second way is to put the author's last name and year in brackets after the referenced work. Known as the **Harvard referencing** system, the full reference must then be written in a bibliography section at the end of your report.

The Harvard referencing system is the most commonly used referencing system, but there are others. There is no requirement to pick any one method. Whichever method you decide to use, it must be clear what sources you have used, and how you have used them.

# Chapter 2
**The report**

### Example of Harvard Referencing

'This piece of text has been taken from a Computer Science book' (Smith, 2019)

The copied text is put in quote marks followed by the author's name and year of publication in brackets. There will then be a full reference at the end of the project which looks like this:

Reeves, J. (2009). *An example Computer Science book title.* Publisher name, pg. 65

Smith, C. (2019). *An example Computer Science book title.* Publisher name, pg. 42

Tapner, B. (2016). *An example Computer Science book title.* Publisher name, pg. 184

*An example of a reference in the bibliography section of the report*

## Using external sources effectively

If you do get stuck during your project, search for techniques and ideas, rather than for complete solutions to your problem. For instance, searching for 'Password Authentication System' and then copying code from a source will limit the marks that can be awarded. However, searching for a technique which can be adapted to your project will allow marks to be gained for the adaptation.

Similarly, a project should not be a record of how you followed a series of online videos to make a game. This will not gain you credit.

| WARNING | Exam boards may use plagiarism checking software. Make sure you reference anything which you have quoted, copied or referred to. |
|---------|--------------------------------------------------------------------------------------------------------------------------------|

# Backups and versions

Your project will be completed over a long period of time and it will take several iterations. It is important to think about the worst-case scenario, such as.

1. Corruption of documents or program code
2. Loss of files on a school network or home computer
3. The need to go back to an older version of the project for evidence or due to issues in a newer version

Many promising projects have been unsuccessful due to students not giving careful thought as to how they will make backups and versions of their work.

| WARNING | Take some time now to think about how you create versions and backup your work at both home and school. |
|---------|---------------------------------------------------------------------------------------------------------|

# Version control

You will complete your project incrementally. Therefore, it makes sense to save versions of your work at regular intervals. This will allow you to go back if you reach a critical error which cannot be corrected. It may allow two potential solutions to a problem to be created to see which works best. It is therefore important to have good **version control** when creating both your report and software.

When using version control ensure that each version is dated. It may also be useful to add a text file which briefly highlights important changes that were made in each version. This will make it easier to find the correct version later.

> **TIP** As a minimum, keep a version of your code at every major iteration and a version of your report after significant work has taken place or a section has been completed.

| Name | Date modified | Type | Size |
|---|---|---|---|
| Project report Ver 1.docx | 15/10/2019 15:55 | Microsoft Word Document | 17 KB |
| Project report Ver 2.docx | 16/10/2019 15:56 | Microsoft Word Document | 92 KB |
| Project report Ver 3.docx | 17/10/2019 12:32 | Microsoft Word Document | 463 KB |

*Different versions of a project report*

# Backups

**Backups** are similar to version control in that multiple backups allow you to keep a record of your work. However, backups need to be kept away from the usual place that you are working. If you work at home, then the backup could be made on the school or college's system. Cloud storage and USB flash drives are other ways to backup work.

**Make sure that there are at least two copies of all your versions of reports and software and that these are stored in at least two different locations.**

How often you choose to backup your work up is up to you, but it is important that it is done. Keeping a full backup of all your work each week is a sensible schedule, however, if you are doing a lot of work on your project, then a daily backup may be a good idea.

> **TASK** Find out what the backup policy is for files at school/college. Plan how you will manage your own version control and backup strategy. Write this below.

School/college backup policy: _____

My backup methods and locations: _____

My backup schedule:_____

# Chapter 2
## The report

## To do list
Have you done the following?

- ☐ Set up a cover page
- ☐ Created a table of contents
- ☐ Created styles for the document (if necessary)
- ☐ Set up your header and footer
- ☐ Created a references section for your report
- ☐ Planned your version and backup strategy

# Chapter 3
## Analysis

## Objectives

- Be able to describe the problem clearly
- Identify your end-user(s) or supervisor
- Research your problem thoroughly
- Use appropriate research methods to collect data including:
  - Product research into similar problems
  - Websites and books
  - Interviews
  - Surveys
  - Making prototypes
- Create a set of objectives for the system that contain the following features:
  - Numbered
  - Specific
  - Measurable
  - Cover all functionality of the solution or areas of investigation
  - Based on dialogue with intended users of the system or supervisor for investigative projects
- Include modelling, diagrams or formulae that will inform the Design section

## The problem

You need to clearly state what the problem is that you are looking to solve. Defining the problem at the start is key to a good project. If you are not sure what is about to be solved, then issues will be encountered later. For instance, it will very difficult to create objectives that are specific and measurable if you are not clear about the problem.

It is good practice to create a clear statement of the problem, the challenges that may be faced and a broad idea of what the system will do.

# Chapter 3
## Analysis

When doing this, think about whether the problem will be too big, or too small. Will it offer enough scope to meet the marking criteria for the project? In particular, will the likely solution allow enough technical skills to be used to be of an A Level standard and access the Group A technical skills?

Be realistic. Well completed 'smaller' projects often score as well as 'larger' projects that may have encountered problems along the way and that are, commonly therefore, not fully functional.

The overall purpose of the Analysis section is to gain a deeper understanding of the problem.

> TASK Create a clear description of the problem you aim to solve.

# Third parties

You will need to identify one or more third parties to be involved with the analysis of your problem. It is likely that this will be an end-user or a group of end-users of the system. See pages 9-13 for more information on how to choose third parties to help.

Remember, some projects will lend themselves to a named end-user who would like to use the solution you create to their problem. However, a project may involve recreating a well-known game such as chess with an AI computer player. In this case, you may choose to use friends, family or chess players for involvement in the analysis section.

If you are carrying out an investigation then you will most likely use your supervisor as your third party for the analysis.

> TASK Identify the person or people who will be involved in your project as a third party. This will typically be your end-user(s) or if you are carrying out an investigation then it will be your supervisor.

# Research

It is important to research the problem you aim to solve thoroughly. All projects should use **research** to help guide and support the requirements of the solution which will be listed in the set of objectives that are created.

Discussions with your end-user(s) or supervisor will need to be undertaken to show the needs of the intended users of the system.

You do not need to undertake all the following types of research. Instead, you should focus on those areas which are most appropriate to the problem or investigation that you are solving or carrying out.

Avoid carrying out research that is irrelevant to your project or investigation. If the below techniques would result in artificial research then don't use them.

## Qualitative and quantitative research

**Qualitative** research produces data which is usually not numerical. This data must be interpreted, rather than putting it into a spreadsheet and trying to make a chart from it.

**Quantitative** research is usually focused on collecting numerical data which can be analysed through calculations or summations.

QUESTION Which of these two questions would give you qualitative data?

*"How do you prefer your interface to look?"*

*"Do you prefer your interface to have green buttons? Yes / No"*

The first answer will be qualitative as there is a wide range of answers that could be given. Once the data is collected, it needs to be interpreted. For example, answers such as "I would like something to click on to process an order" and "There should be an easy way to create an order" could be interpreted as "Button to process an order".

The second question is quantitative. There are only two answers, Yes or No. It would be possible to ask a number of stakeholders which they prefer and then analyse the data in a spreadsheet or with a chart.

## Researching other solutions

Analysing other solutions and software is a great way to get ideas about how the problem could be solved. These systems will be solving a similar problem to the one which you are tackling. For instance, if you are making a 2D platform game, there are hundreds of existing games that could be used to show your end users and get feedback on. They could be shown anything from gameplay, interfaces, graphics style or game themes and then comment on them.

When evidencing the research from other solutions, it is possible to include screenshots, diagrams or explanations of the solution. In some cases, it is then appropriate to add your own comments as to what you like or don't like. This can then be linked to how it informed your objectives. The comments or views of your end-users are also very useful.

It may be that you think your idea is unique and that no other comparable systems exist. If this really is the case, then you should find systems that are as similar as possible or take different components from other systems that solve parts of your problem.

For example, a project requires a new game to be created using dice, cards and marbles. It is based around players taking turns with dice, and then battling with cards. The winner collects marbles that allow them to power-up either the dice or the cards.

In this case, you could research other card battling games such as Top Trumps® or Pokémon® for card designs and a description of the gameplay. Other games may then give ideas as to how the interface could look on a computer screen.

The same principle applies to any problem being researched and its potential solution. There will always be avenues of research which can influence your requirements list.

If appropriate to your problem or investigation, identify other software or solutions that solve something similar to the problem you have or components of the solution you will be proposing. Include screenshots and diagrams where appropriate.

Analyse the solutions you have chosen. What are their strengths or weaknesses? How could they be adapted for your solution? What opinions do your end-users or supervisor have?

# Interviews

Meeting your end-user(s) or supervisor is a great way to gain information. It also has drawbacks.

| Benefits | Drawbacks |
|---|---|
| • Able to talk to people directly | • You may need to travel |
| • Guaranteed meeting time | • They may be hard to get hold of |
| • You can ask questions that you may not have thought of before the meeting | • They may be very busy |
| • You can ask them for more detail instantly | • They may not give you as much time as you had hoped, meaning the meeting is rushed |
| • You can get a better understanding of your stakeholders and their problem | • You need to be confident speaking to people face to face |
| • You can build a relationship more easily | • They may cancel at the last minute leading to delays in your research |
| • They may feel more confident in the project after meeting you | • Too many meetings with one stakeholder may put them off |

Balancing whether to meet end-users or not depends on many considerations. You may decide to meet a key end-user, but then use a questionnaire or email for other third parties. For instance, in a system involving a manager and other administration staff, it may be beneficial to meet the manager for a discussion, but easier to collect information from the administration staff using a survey.

*Meetings with your stakeholder(s) are
essential to understand the problem*

TIP
Meetings take a lot of time to set up, but often get better quality data. Balance this with the effort required in organising many meetings and make each one worthwhile and focused.

Remember that the key part of the Analysis is that you are having a dialogue with your end-user(s) or supervisor. Whilst meetings are a great way to do this, in some cases, email, phone calls or other online communication methods may be easier to organise and therefore more appropriate.

TASK
Set up at least one meeting with your main end-user or a group of end-users to discuss the problem. Record any ideas they have for the solution and any questions or points that have arisen in your research into other solutions. If you are carrying out an investigation be sure to record key ideas that arise from meeting your supervisor.

# Chapter 3
## Analysis

## Surveys

Surveys are a way of collecting data without needing to be present. They can be quickly created and are simple to send out, but they can be difficult to design well.

| Benefits | Drawbacks |
|---|---|
| • Able to send to many people at once<br>• Stakeholders can complete in their own time<br>• May allow for quicker data capture<br>• You can ask a range of questions<br>• You can do them electronically or on paper<br>• It may be easier to move into other software to analyse if done electronically<br>• Some questionnaire platforms analyse data for you | • You must be sure you ask the right questions<br>• Designing your questionnaire takes skill and time<br>• People may miss the email or link<br>• You will need to chase people to complete it<br>• You cannot clarify questions immediately<br>• You cannot always be sure all of the data entered is accurate<br>• Paper-based surveys need collating |

Electronic surveys are very effective if you want to collect data from a large number of people, and the questions you want to ask are all the same for everyone. For example, if you are creating a game and need 20 people to answer some questions, a survey would be a great approach to take.

Designing a survey is challenging and not as easy as it first seems. However, many survey platforms have builders in them to help you create a good survey and test how effective it is before sending it out.

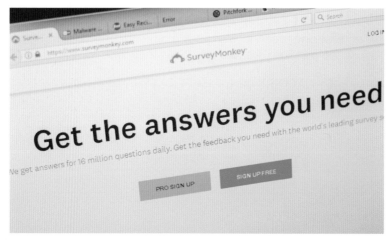

*SurveyMonkey® is a free survey creator*

> **TIP** When designing a survey, make sure you ask high-quality questions which gather the data you want to know.

Generally, it is more likely that you will use interviews first, and then follow up surveys to help clarify points and ideas you get from meetings. However, there is no right or wrong way.

It is important that you look at the time both you and your end-user(s) have available and plan appropriately. If you have questions for just one person it may be quicker to prepare a list of questions, and then ask them in a phone call, web conference, or Skype™ call instead of a meeting.

> ### TASK
>
> If appropriate to your problem or investigation, choose whether you need to use surveys, questionnaires, or voice/video calls. Then plan how you will both analyse the results and then follow these up afterwards.

## Prototyping

Prototyping is used when your initial idea is formed, but the requirements are very vague and undefined. Prototyping allows you to build short and quick examples, which can be evaluated and refined as you go. This may then lead to an iterative design once you have more idea as to the direction of the project.

Prototyping can achieve a working skeleton product very quickly. It is important to remember that this will not necessarily lead to a final, defined product. However, it will help in defining the final product, and give you useful feedback.

Prototypes are a useful way of developing small parts of the program that are crucial to the final solution. For a route-finding program, this may be the key algorithm for finding routes. For a program that relies on an online database accessed from an app, it may be a simple prototype that demonstrates that you can connect to the database from the app.

> ### TIP
>
> Tackle the core part of the project that the rest depends on first. Developing the first iterations or prototypes early will mean that you won't have a major stumbling block late in the project.

Be aware that prototyping is part of the Analysis section as it is helping to inform the objectives. It will help to demonstrate that critical parts of the project are achievable and it may lead to more than one approach that can be discussed with end-user(s) or a supervisor.

If you create prototypes, it is important that you have a point where you stop their development once critical problems have been solved. This allows you to then create a set of achievable objectives for the development of your technical solution.

# Modelling of the problem

There are times when you may wish to show models, diagrams or formulae that are key to the problem. The types of models and diagrams that are used may be similar to those discussed in the Design section, however, if they directly relate to, or aid in the understanding of, the problem, then they should be included at this point.

# Chapter 3
## Analysis

The following table shows some example situations where you may wish to show models, diagrams or formulae that are key to understanding the problem.

| Problem | Modelling that may be required in the Analysis section |
|---|---|
| • To design an online system that allows people to record their family tree and collaborate/join it to other user's trees | • A tree diagram or network graph would be useful to see the structures that would be created by the problem |
| • A burglar alarm system that detects types of alarm and assesses their threat level before alerting the owner | • A state diagram to show the states of the alarm system |
| • A teaching tool to explain planet orbits | • Equations/laws that govern the motion of planets |
| • A tracking tool for a teacher responsible for trips that keep a record of the process and documents required | • A flow diagram to show the decisions that are taken in the process |
| • An investigation into crime trends using public data | • An E-R model showing the entities and relationships of data sets that have been found<br>• Equations/theories that relate to crime trends |

# Project objectives

The set of **objectives** you create define the requirements for the rest of the project. Each objective should have some sort of research to support its inclusion in your project. One way to show that research supports inclusion is to make a note as you do the research. For example, when writing down points from a meeting with an end-user you could highlight key parts and state that they will need to be included in the objectives.

When writing your set of objectives, it is important to include some sort of numbering for each one. This will help you to reference them later in the project. It is useful, for each objective, to refer back to evidence in your research that justifies it.

WARNING

The set of objectives you produce is the most important part of your Analysis section. It immediately reveals what you are setting out to do in the project and will be used to determine how successful your solution is. In addition to this, it will inform your marker and moderator as to whether this is a project that is of A level standard. It is likely that a moderator will turn to your objectives first in order to establish what you are setting out to achieve and how challenging it is.

One way to develop the set of objectives is to start with the most important ones and then break them down into smaller ones.

The following is an extract from a set of objectives for a website that allows parents to book parents' evening appointments.

4. Parents need to be informed of the appointments that they have just made.
    4.1. Once they have confirmed the appointment a page will be displayed which contains:
        4.1.1. The appointment times
        4.1.2. The names of the teachers
        4.1.3. The subject for each teacher
    4.2. A print button will be on the confirmation page. When clicked this will print all the appointment details given in objective 4.1
    4.3. An automated email will be sent to them with details of the appointment given in objective 4.1 and a link that enables them to change it
5. Admin staff need to be able to look up appointments for a parent. This may be carried out on behalf of a teacher request or parent contacting the school.
    5.1. Admin staff will be able to put a student's name into a search box
    5.2. This will then find all the appointments that their parents have made (same details as 4.1)
    5.3. Admin staff can carry out the following appointment functions:
        5.3.1. Add new appointments
        5.3.2. Edit existing appointments
        5.3.3. Delete appointments
    5.4. When the admin staff click the "Confirm changes" button the new appointments are sent in a confirmation email to the parent

*Example of a section of a set of objectives*

# Chapter 3
## Analysis

| TIP | Break down the requirements into sections which then have small, specific and measurable objectives. |

## Objectives for investigations

Investigations are often harder to write objectives for. It is crucial that the objectives created for investigations are also specific and measurable. This does not prevent them from allowing further investigation at further stages of the project.

For example, imagine a project was looking into computer-generated graphics and using an Art teacher as a supervisor.

An objective of 'Create a piece of art' would be far too broad and impossible to measure. Not only would it reduce the mark for the Analysis section but it would make it hard to achieve marks in the following sections.

The following shows an extract from some objectives that are more specific and measurable whilst allowing an investigation to still take place.

1. The pictures produced by the software should try to produce computer-generated images of countryside landscapes.
    1.1. It should make use of repeated features in objects, emphasising their fractal nature
        1.1.1. Recursion should be considered to repeat elements of the image
    1.2. Images should consider colour schemes that make use of complementary colours
    1.3. The composition of the landscape needs to be considered
        1.3.1. The image should obey the rule of thirds where possible – so key parts should line up in thirds or be at an intersection of thirds
        1.3.2. The image should appear natural – e.g. trees must not be growing in rivers and rivers must not be placed at the top of hills, but in valleys

| TIP | If some of your objectives go further than A Level standard requirements then you can mark these as extension objectives. You will not lose marks if you do not implement these. Discuss with your teacher if you think that you may have extension objectives. |

> **TASK**
>
> Create a list of numbered objectives for your system. Start with the main ones, and then break each main area into smaller ones. Make sure that the objectives reflect the needs that were identified earlier in your dialogue with your end-user(s) or supervisor.

# Commentary

Your commentary throughout your report should take both your teacher and the moderator through the journey to reach your final solution. It is not a specific section but runs through the whole project. Commentaries are written explanations of what, when and why you are doing something.

Quality is more important than quantity so be concise. Avoid writing 100 words when 10 would do.

Commentary for the Analysis section should show how you went from an initial idea for a problem, researched it, discussed it with your end-user(s) or supervisor, and reached your final decision for the solution.

## To do list
Have you done the following?

- [ ] Created a clear description of the problem being solved/investigated

- [ ] Identified the end-users/supervisor that will be used in the project

- [ ] Researched products/software for similar problems (if appropriate for your project)

- [ ] Researched relevant websites and books (if appropriate for your project)

- [ ] Carried out interviews, discussion, communication or dialogue with your end-user(s)/supervisor

- [ ] Carried out surveys/questionnaires with end-user(s) or other third parties (if appropriate for your project)

- [ ] Made prototypes of key/critical areas (if appropriate for your project)

- [ ] Given enough detail that a third party would understand the problem being solved/investigated

- [ ] Added or created models/diagrams/formulae that can be used to inform the Design section

- [ ] Created a list of numbered objectives which are specific, measurable and cover all required functionality of the solution/areas of investigation

# Chapter 4
## Documented design

## Objectives

- Understand the purpose of the Documented Design section
- Where appropriate create the following designs:
    - Structure/hierarchy chart
    - System flowchart
    - Data flow diagram (DFD)
    - Database design
    - Database queries
    - Entity-Relationship (E-R) diagrams
    - Algorithms
    - Data structures
    - File structures
    - HCI (Human-Computer Interaction)/Screen designs
    - Hardware selection

## What is Documented design?

Before programming code or a solution is implemented, it needs to be designed. This can, for instance, take the form of diagrams, charts, algorithms or screen designs.

Whilst it is likely that some of your solution will be designed before any implementation takes place, AQA accepts that it is most likely that you will use an iterative methodology. As such, it may be that once you have coded one part or iteration of the project you then start the next design or a re-design of something that didn't work well. This is perfectly acceptable. Whilst your actual designs may occur at many different stages in the project, they are all put into the Documented design section of your report. Hence it is called 'Documented design' and not just Design. This book will refer to this section as the Documented design section and Design section interchangeably.

It is important that your Design section gives an overview of how the different parts of the solution interact.

Before putting any diagrams into your report, it is important to give a textual overview which summarises the key components required.

> **TIP**
> Remember that textual overviews to introduce diagrams and tables will be very helpful for your teacher and moderator when reading your report.

> **TASK**
> Write an overview of the design of your project as a whole. Remember to also write a textual overview of any diagrams that you create later in the Design section.

One of more of the following design methods will help to achieve this:
- Structure/hierarchy chart
- System flowchart
- Data flow diagram (DFD)
- Object/class diagram

Once you have given an overview of the design of the system, you then need to show how specific key parts of it work. This can be carried out using any methods that are appropriate. Design methods that are often used include the following:
- Database design
- Database queries
- Entity-Relationship (E-R) diagrams
- Algorithms
- Data structures
- File structures
- HCI (Human-Computer Interaction)/Screen designs
- Hardware selection

> **TIP**
> You do not need to include all the above design methods. Instead, you should choose those that are applicable to your project. The designs that you produce should fully articulate what is required in the solution.

If your project requires more depth on a small number of technical areas, then the designs will need to have more depth than a project that makes use of many technical areas.

Your Design section is not limited to the above design methods. If there are other diagrams that are appropriate then you can use these, especially where they use industry-standard methods.

The following sections cover the more common design methods listed above. They are a primer on the topic so that you can see if the design method fits your project. You may need to cover these in more depth than shown in this book. If so, research further from your A level course and other sources.

# Structure/hierarchy diagrams

Your project will involve producing a substantial amount of program code. The problem will be too large to simply start coding the solution immediately.

**Decomposition** is the technical term for splitting a large problem into smaller ones. Many people want to start programming far too early in the project. However, once errors arise or the approach changes, it can become very challenging to manage the code.

> TIP
>
> Remember that textual overviews to introduce diagrams and tables will be very helpful for your teacher and moderator when reading your report.

Once you have split the problem up, it becomes easier to track progress through it. The smaller the parts, the easier they may be to solve and manage.

Many word processing packages have tools which can be used to create structure diagrams. The diagrams shown below were created using tools within Microsoft® Word®.

One method of showing a structure is shown below, but you could use other diagrams, charts or layouts. Remember that these diagrams are only examples and your diagram is likely to contain more information.

Whilst these diagrams can be easy to create, careful consideration should be made at this stage so that the problem is decomposed into meaningful parts.

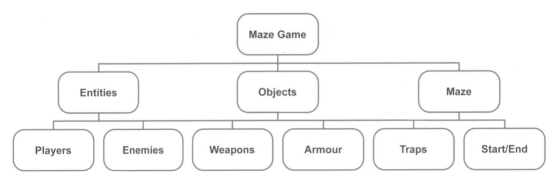

*Example 1 – Structure diagram for a maze game*

## Hand-drawn drawings

If you prefer, you can draw decomposition diagrams by hand. These can then be photographed or scanned and added to the report. However, remember that drawing by hand can take longer and be harder to make changes to later. Be aware that if your solution changes or you decide to restructure later, you will need to redraw the diagrams again. This is likely to be harder with a hand-drawn diagram unless the alteration is small.

> **TASK** If appropriate for your project, create a structure/hierarchy diagram that shows how you have decomposed your problem.

# System flowcharts

A system flowchart allows a third party to see very quickly an overview of how the system works. The symbols used are similar to those used in flow charts for algorithms. At this level, though, remember that the diagram is showing an overview of the system. Algorithms can be shown using flowcharts or pseudocode later.

The key symbols used are as follows :

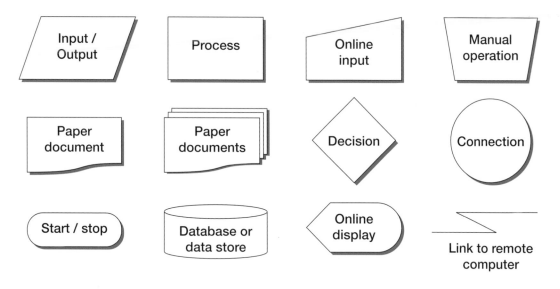

# Chapter 4
## Documented design

The following example shows part of a system flowchart for registration with an online booking system.

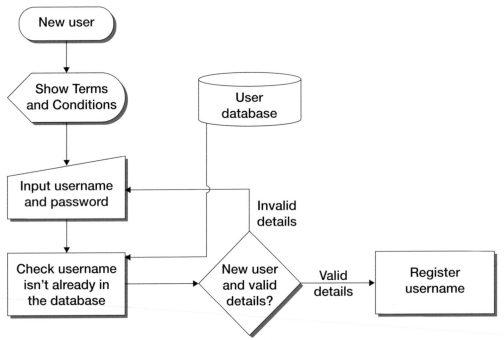

*An example of a section of a system flowchart*

> **TASK** If appropriate for your project, create a system flowchart that gives an overview of how the key processes in your system work.

## Data Flow Diagrams

**Data Flow Diagrams (DFDs)** show the inputs, outputs and how data moves within your system.

Datastores are the databases or files within the system. In the analysis, the users of the system will have been identified along with the actions which they will carry out.

Here is an example of a very simple Data Flow Diagram for a student registering on to a course in a school:

This shows that a student would pass their details to a process called 'Enrol on Course'. This process would then store the details in the 'Course' database.

A DFD for a school management system would be much more complicated in real life. DFDs may be time-consuming to draw but will help to show how data moves within your system.

DFDs will require more understanding of database design. This, linked with how long they may take to design, should be a consideration. If your system is very simple, you may decide a simple E-R Diagram will be sufficient.

| TIP | There are many diagrams that can help with the design of databases. Doing all of these for a large system may take a lot of time. You may wish to discuss with your teacher how much depth you need to go into to perform well. |
|---|---|

| TASK | If appropriate for your project, create a DFD to show how data will flow through your system. |
|---|---|

# Object-oriented design

**Object-oriented design** looks at creating entities known as objects which interact with each other. Each object can interact with another object, but only in specific ways.

**Object-Oriented Programming (OOP)** focuses on core ideas:

- **Inheritance** to help reusability
- **Polymorphism** for flexibility
- **Encapsulation** to keep states and behaviours within each object

If you plan on designing an object-orientated program, you must ensure that you develop the skills to do so. Object-oriented programming is part of the A Level specification. It is likely that most systems you create will tend to favour an object-oriented design, but not all will.

The following section looks at some of the key terminology and concepts of object-oriented programming.

## Building Object-Oriented designs

Object orientation requires you to be able to spot common areas in parts of your problem that need a class to implement them.

### Classes

**Classes** will be created as a 'template' for objects that you can identify within your design. For example, in a car racing game a `Car` would be one class which would store attributes such as `currentSpeed` and `maximumSpeed` along with methods (also known as behaviours) such as `increaseSpeed()` or `decreaseSpeed()`.

# Chapter 4
## Documented design

`Player` may be another class that stores information such as `playerName` and `score`.

The methods may be `getName()`, `setName(name)`, `addScore(amount)` and `getScore()`.

Looking at your decomposition may help to find areas of your problem that can make up different classes.

In object-oriented programming, the terms we use change a little from procedural programming.

| Procedural programming | Object-oriented programming |
|---|---|
| Variables | Attributes |
| Procedures / functions | Methods |

## Objects

A class can be used to create multiple instances known as **objects**. This is known as an **instantiation** of a class.

Remember that the class forms a template that is re-used in making each object/instance. In the previous example of a car racing game, if three players played the game, there would be three instances of the `Player` class created for each of them. Each instance could have the same attributes and methods as the `Player` class. Each instance could then store a unique `playerName` and score for each given player.

> **TIP** Classes can be thought of as categories with objects being the specific instances. For instance, `Person` would be a class, whilst `Bob` and `Alice` would be instances.

## Sub-classes

A class will match a certain category such as a `Car` class. It may be possible to make sub-categories from this. These are known as sub-classes. In the car game, the `Car` class stores `currentSpeed` and `maximumSpeed` as two attributes. Sub-classes could then be created for `PoliceCar`, `SportsCar` and `Taxi`. Each of these sub-classes would **inherit** these attributes, so they would each store the `currentSpeed` and `maximumSpeed`. The sub-classes could also have their own unique attributes and methods though. For example, the `PoliceCar` sub-class could have an attribute for `sirenState` with the methods `sirenOn()` and `sirenOff()`.

The ability of a sub-class to inherit attributes or methods from its **parent** class is known as **inheritance**.

> **QUESTION** A quiz game is to be designed for a school classroom that one or more students and teachers can play. Any teacher can ask a question and any student can then respond. How could classes and sub-classes be used in the solution?

A class could be made called `Person`. This might store the `name` of each person and the time that they join the game `(timeJoined)` as attributes. The methods might be `getTimeJoined()`, `getName()` and `setName()`.

Two sub-classes could then be created. The `Teacher` sub-class might contain the method `setQuestion(question)`. The `Student` sub-class may have the method `answerQuestion(answer)`.

Both Teacher and Student would inherit the methods and attributes from the Person class, so they would also be able to use the methods `getTimeJoined()`, `getName()` and `setName()`.

## Identifying Objects, Attributes and Behaviours

### Identifying Objects

Objects are often the nouns in your system. Take an estate agent for example. House, Agent and Buyer are all nouns and could well form classes or sub-classes.

### Identifying Attributes

Attributes may also be called properties or class variables. Attributes store the values that are encapsulated in an object. Attributes of a House would be things such as `numberOfBedrooms` and `price`. Attributes will be shown inside a class on a class diagram.

### Identifying Behaviours

Behaviours are the methods that a Class can perform. A behaviour of the `Agent` class may be 'Sell House'. This may be implemented by the method `sellHouse()`. Behaviours of the `Buyer` class may be `setMaxPrice()` and `setMinPrice()`.

> **TIP** Remember that OOP design is a broad subject and other sources of information will go into more depth on the subject.

## Class diagrams

Class diagrams are a standard way of showing an object-oriented design. They are drawn using **Unified Modelling Language (UML)**.

Class diagrams will show you:
1. Each of the classes used
2. The attributes available within each class
3. The methods available within each class
4. Whether classes are sub-classes, and inherit attributes and methods from a parent class

UML has many notations within it and an in-depth look is beyond the scope of this book. However, there are many websites available giving tutorials and explanations of UML.

The basic building block of a class diagram is an individual class.

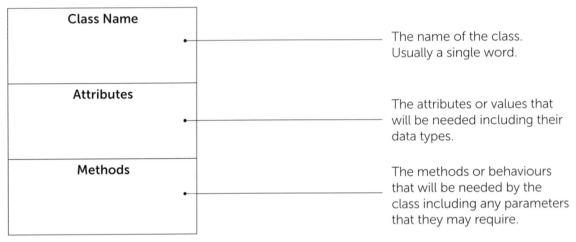

| Class Name | |
|---|---|
| | The name of the class. Usually a single word. |
| **Attributes** | The attributes or values that will be needed including their data types. |
| **Methods** | The methods or behaviours that will be needed by the class including any parameters that they may require. |

*The layout of a class*

> **TIP** It is highly advisable that you have solved some simple programming problems in an OOP style before you attempt to write your own class diagrams.

## Worked example of class diagrams

This worked example will consider a battleships style game and assume that the initial analysis of the problem has already been carried out.

First, start with a class diagram for the Ship class:

| Ship |
| --- |
| shipType : String<br>shipLength : int<br>shipLocation: int[]<br>shipOrientation: Char |
| setOrientation: Char<br>setShipLocation(int[])<br>getShipType()<br>getShipLength()<br>getShipLocation()<br>getShipOrientation()<br>hitShip(int[]) |

*An example of one class*

**WARNING** — The diagrams shown in this section are examples only and do not form a full system.

This diagram shows us that we need to create a class called Ship. It will have four attributes which store the data for the type of the ship, the length of the ship, the location of the ship and its orientation which will be either horizontal or vertical.

Each attribute has a data type shown in the diagram and includes a string, an integer, an array of integers and a Boolean type.

There are two methods shown for setting the attributes. These methods are very simple and just allow the values stored in the attributes to be changed. They also show the parameters that may need to be passed to the methods. hitShip(location) by contrast, is a method that can be called when the ship is hit. The class diagram doesn't show the algorithm that will be used for the methods, but it does show what methods the class will need to have programmed.

Symbols can be placed before each of the attributes or methods in a class diagram to show whether they are public (+), private (-) or protected (#).

# Chapter 4
## Documented design

## Sub-classes and inheritance

There are different types of ship in the game. These include a carrier, battleship and submarine. Each of these ships will have many of the same features as the `Ship` class, so we can use inheritance to create subclasses. The subclasses will have all the same attributes and methods of the parent class, but they can also add new ones that are unique to the particular subclass.

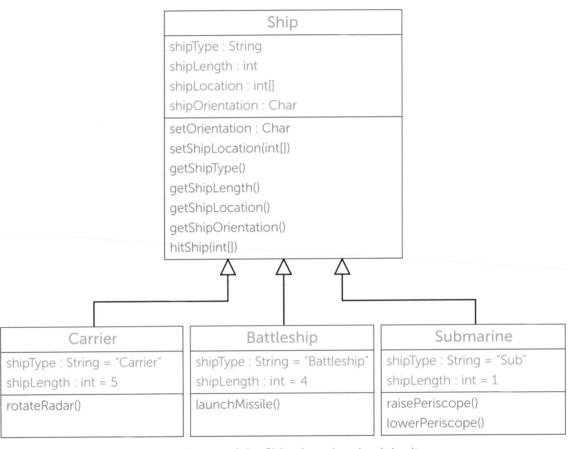

*Three subclasses of the Ship class showing inheritance*

## Association links and multiplicity

A `Board` class can be added which will store where ships are placed and control what happens when they are hit. 1 board has exactly 5 ships, so these numbers can be written by the **association link**. Note that in the real game, two boards would be needed, one for each player.

| Ship | | 5 ——————————— 1 | | Board |
|---|---|---|---|---|

| Ship |
|---|
| shipType : String |
| shipLength : int |
| shipLocation : int[] |
| shipOrientation : Char |
| setOrientation : Char |
| setShipLocation(int[]) |
| getShipType() |
| getShipLength() |
| getShipLocation() |
| getShipOrientation() |
| hitShip(int[]) |

| Board |
|---|
| boardName : String |
| gameboard : String[12,12] |
| currentPlayerTurn : String |
| swapPlayer() |
| addShip(ship,x,y) |
| hit(x,y) |
| updateDisplay() |

The number of instances that are created from each class is known as **multiplicity**.

| 0..1 | No instances or one instance |
|---|---|
| 1 | Exactly one instance |
| 0..* | Zero or more instances |
| 1..* | One or more instances |
| * | Any number of instances |
| 4..6 | 4 to 6 instances |
| 3 | Exactly 3 instances |

*Possible multiplicity instances*

Further classes would need to be built for other objects in the game such as the players.

 **TASK** If your project will make use of object-oriented programming techniques then create a class diagram to describe the system.

Note that the AQA specification expects a broader understanding of OOP than that given above. If your project is heavily using OOP then when creating any designs you should consider which of the following key aspects are relevant to your project.

- Classes
- Encapsulation
- Composition
- Interfaces

- Objects
- Inheritance
- Polymorphism
- Abstract, virtual and static methods

- Instantiation
- Aggregation
- Overriding
- Public (+), private (-) and protected (#) specifiers

# Database design

Many systems will rely on a database to store data. Design the database structure or schema before it is built.

> **TIP** For more complex databases, you must understand the relevant database theory such as normalisation before you design the structure.

There are some key considerations to designing databases:

1.  ## Data storage
    Although a project may need to store data, it doesn't mean that a database is required. Some data storage could be done through a simple file storage method. However, systems such as stock storage, orders and bookings will likely need the more complex facilities of a database.

2.  ## Data relationships
    If the database required has more than one table then it is likely that there will be relationships between the data. Most database designs will need to be **normalised** to remove **data redundancy**.

3.  ## Database-program connections
    There must be a way to connect your main program to the database. In some cases this is easy, but in others, it may be more complex. You will also need to be confident in writing SQL statements for database queries.

4.  ## Database design
    Database design will require the creation of one or more **Entity Relationship (E-R) diagrams**.

# SQL

SQL stands for **Structured Query Language**. Knowledge of this language will be needed in order to access data from a database.

Some **Relational Database Management Systems (RDBMS)** allow you to design your databases through a GUI. A popular example is Microsoft® Access®.

Remember that SQL isn't considered a *programming* language. It is a **query language** which can be used in your project, but you must make use of a text language such as C#, VB or Python. Use languages such as these to connect to a database if one is required. SQL can then be used to make necessary queries to the database.

> **TIP** The use of several tables, SQL queries that take parameters and also the SQL required to create the tables are all Group A technical skills.

## SQL syntax

A full consideration of SQL is beyond the scope of this book, however, some key terms are given below for reference.

| SQL Command | Meaning | SQL Command | Effect |
|---|---|---|---|
| **SELECT** | Selects specific records from the table that meet certain criteria | **OR** | For a match, one or the other criteria are needed |
| **FROM** | Identifies which table the records will come from | **DELETE** | Used to delete data from a database table |
| **WHERE** | Adds the criteria that records returned need to meet | **INSERT INTO** | Used to add data to a database table |
| **LIKE** | Used to match patterns with the wildcards % (for zero, one or many characters) and _ (for a single character) | **JOIN** | Allows you to select data from multiple tables at once |
| **AND** | For a match, both criteria are needed | **UPDATE** | Allows records to be updated – used with the SET keyword |

# Chapter 4
## Documented design

## Parameterised SQL

Basic queries tend to be written in the style:

SELECT column1, column2, column3 FROM TableName WHERE criteria

For example:

```
SELECT customerID, name FROM Sales WHERE spend > amountRequested
```

Although the above SQL query shows the use of the parameter amountRequested, it only uses one table. As such, it would only be demonstrating a Group B skill.

To demonstrate a Group A skill, parameterised SQL statements that use more than one table should be written where appropriate.

For example:

```
SELECT Customers.name, Orders.total
FROM Customers
JOIN Orders ON Customers.customerID=Orders.CustomerID
WHERE spend > amountRequested
```

## Additional SQL features

If your project relies heavily on databases and SQL then you should aim to use both Aggregate SQL functions and a script to create and initialise the database (DDL script).

Aggregate SQL functions perform basic calculations on data. The most commonly used of these are given in the below table.

| Aggregate function | Meaning |
| --- | --- |
| Count(*) | Returns the number of records |
| Count(productType) | Returns the number of distinct values for productType |
| sum(salary) | Finds the total of a column |
| Avg(salary) | Finds the average of a column |
| Min(salary) | Finds the minimum value in a column |
| Max(salary) | Finds the maximum value in a column |

A DDL script is where a Data Definition Language has been used in a script to create the tables and other parts of the data model for a database. The script can be made using SQL and the following commands will be useful to research when doing this:

- CREATE DATABASE databasename;
- CREATE TABLE tableName ( col1 datatype, col2 datatype,…);

There is also SQL statements that can specify if fields are primary keys, autoincrement or should not be null.

 **TASK** If you will be using a database to store data, create designs for the key queries that will be used.

## Multi-table databases

At A Level, you are likely to need a multi-table database and the use of several tables is a Group A technical skill. The tables will need to be normalised and typically will be in **3rd Normal Form (3NF)**. Both SQL and Normalisation are topics within the A Level specification.

Both SQL and Normalisation are topics within the A Level specification.

Carefully consider the database design before any implementation. Well organised data can be retrieved easily and help your program to work effectively.

## Data tables

Data tables will show the core properties of each field in your database, as well as the table name and keys used. Each table should have a data table associated with it.

There are several important things to show in your data tables:

1. Table name
2. Field names
3. Primary key
4. Any secondary or foreign keys
5. Data types
6. Validation

Data tables can be set up quite easily in a word processor as the following example shows:

**Table: Customer**

| Field | Key | Data Type | Validation | Notes |
|---|---|---|---|---|
| Customer_ID | Primary | Number | | |
| Name | | String | 1-20 | |
| Surname | | String | 1-40 | |
| Address | | String | 1-100 | |
| Date_Of_Birth | | Date/Time | <TODAY () | |
| Postcode | | String | 5-8 chars Input Mask | |
| Email | | String | >5 Include '@' | |

*An example of a data table for a Customer table*

TASK: If you will be using a database to store data, create a data table for each table you will need. You may also wish to demonstrate how you have normalised the data into 3NF.

## Entity-relationship diagrams

**Entity-Relationship (E-R)** diagrams should be made for any database that will be created.

The minimum requirement for an Entity Relationship diagram will be that it shows all the **entities** (tables) and the **relationships** between them. Relationships will be given as **one-to-one**, **one-to-many** and **many-to-many**. E-R diagrams can also contain **attributes** (field names) that are associated with particular entities.

The following example is a simple E-R diagram for an ordering system. A customer has one order which contains many line items. Each order line contains a single item but an item may be ordered more than once on a different line or a different order.

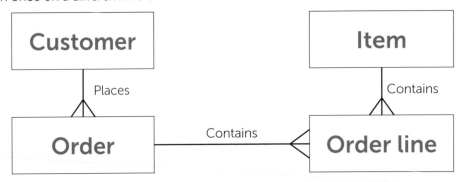

*A simple E-R diagram for an online ordering system*

> TASK   If you will be using a database to store data, create an E-R diagram.

# Algorithms

It is important that all **algorithms** for the solution are designed accurately and appropriately. You only need to show a sample of key algorithms that are to be used in the program. The algorithms that you choose may be created by you, or be standard algorithms that you have found, such as an A* pathfinding algorithm or a method to sort a binary tree.

The algorithms will demonstrate how the more challenging or essential parts of your project work. They will also be used as evidence of the technical difficulty of your solution.

> TIP   Trivial algorithms do not need to be planned or evidenced. Instead, spend time planning algorithms for key or challenging parts of the system.

# Algorithm design

Algorithms can be described in a number of different ways. Typically, a style of pseudocode that is similar to program code will be the easiest to use later in the implementation stage.

Some complex algorithms may require explanations of how they work in English or a flow chart to make them easier to understand. However, typically you will only need to use one of the following methods for your algorithm designs.

> **TIP** The method used to show algorithms for the solutions is up to you. What is important is that the algorithms presented are appropriate and accurate.

The following are examples of how algorithms can be shown in the Design section for a simple algorithm that will multiply two numbers together. This algorithm is purposefully very simple to show the different styles that can be used to present it. The algorithms you produce will be far more complex.

You may find that algorithms created in pseudocode are the fastest to write and translate to the programming language which you are using.

### Algorithm using structured English

> This algorithm will need to take two numbers as inputs and multiply them together. The result will then be returned to the main program.

### Algorithm using a flow diagram

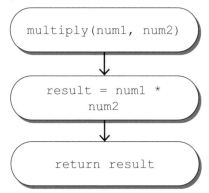

### Algorithm using pseudocode

```
function multiply(num1:int, num2:int)
    result = num1 * num2
    return result
end multiply
```

# Chapter 4
## Documented design

TIP     Try to use monospaced fonts when writing pseudocode.

### Improving algorithms

If you are developing your programs iteratively, you may find that the algorithm changes significantly from your first ideas. Whether the algorithm is simplified or becomes more complicated, it is important to record the changes in the design and the reasons for the changes. This will help with demonstrating excellent coding style in the solution that is created.

TIP     The symbols used for flow diagrams must be used correctly. There is, however, no standard pseudocode style. The pseudocode that you write should be written in a manner that can easily be understood by another programmer.

TASK     Create algorithms that describe the solution fully. These must be appropriate and accurate. Justify how these algorithms form a complete solution to the problem.

# Data structures and advanced techniques

Identifying and justifying your use of data structures will often be a significant aspect of the design section.

Your Design section should, where possible, demonstrate your use of technical skills from Group A below. Other data structures from Groups B and C are worth adding to your report if they add to the clarity and understanding of your designs.

| Group A | Group B | Group C |
| --- | --- | --- |
| Hash tables | Multi-dimensional arrays | Single-dimensional arrays |
| Lists / linked lists | Dictionaries | Variables |
| Stacks | Records | Simple datatypes (e.g. integer / real / Boolean) |
| Queues | | |
| Graphs | | |
| Trees | | |

Each of these data structures has standard ways of being represented. If your project requires these structures, show the structure and then illustrate it in your report with sample data as necessary.

TIP     You only need to mention those data structures or variables that are part of the critical or ingenious parts of your solution. Listing all variables in your program is NOT necessary and will waste your time.

Remember that you need to justify your decisions. For instance, the use of a queue may be appropriate to determine the next player in a game due to the way the data structure provides the facility to add (enqueue) a new player to the queue and remove (dequeue) the player at the front of the queue.

Justifications for other data structures, classes or databases may include the simplicity of the program required, speed of execution or requirements for re-usability.

Some programming languages may already have libraries for data structures that are needed. Show how you will use these, and how they will support your system.

How much evidence you need will depend on your project. For instance, a solution that makes heavy use of databases, server-side scripting and object-oriented programming is likely to have already demonstrated more than enough evidence of Group A skills. Further documenting of data structures is therefore only required if they are key to the solution or aid the understanding of the solution.

 TASK Identify key data structures that will be used in your system. Remember to include algorithms that demonstrate the more challenging technical skills required in your project.

# File structures

A file structure shows how you plan to arrange files into folders or directories. The following is a simple example file structure for a dynamic website.

```
-settings.txt
-public_html
    -javascript
    -images
    -css
    -admin
        -index.php
    -index.php
    -search.php
    -results.php
```

For many apps and software programs, the file structures will be very easy to understand and can be described to aid understanding of the files and directories in the program.

For dynamic websites and applications, file structures may become more complex. Indeed, it is possible for queries to appear as a directory structure.

For example, the URL: https://www.anexamplesite.com/news/nov/18, may in fact not have directories for news, nov or 18. Instead, these may be converted to GET parameters that are interpreted by a server-side script. In this case, the taxonomy should be designed that shows how areas of the site are classified and grouped together.

Alternatively, your solution or investigation may be saving files. For instance, if mapping data for cities were being saved with a certain file format and filename format, then you would need to explain this.

> **TASK** If your project relies on more files, then show how the file structure will be organised.

# HCI (Human-Computer Interaction) / Screen designs

Designs should be given for any point where the user interacts with the computer. Typically this will be a screen design, and almost all projects require some on-screen interaction.

When designing a Graphical User Interface (GUI), you should consider the placement of all GUI objects. For example, in a game, this may be the menu system and placement of objects such as health bars and scores. For other systems, it may be where users enter data, view results and have menu bars placed.

The GUI is an important part of a project and should be accurately sketched out.

> **TIP** You should have researched features of GUIs for similar software to that which you are designing in the Analysis section. Make sure your designs reference any applicable research that was carried out earlier.

Wireframes are a good way of designing your GUI. These are line drawings. They will help to show key features and layout clearly. Specific aspects can be numbered and explained in more detail.

If you have key themes or **house styles** that must be used in the requirements specification, then refer to these here.

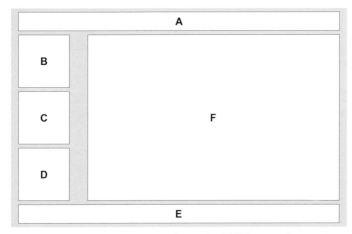

A: Page header

**B, C, D**: Advertising

E: Page Footer

F: Page Content

**Styles**
Header:
- Arial Bold 14pt, Blue

Page text:
- Arial 12pt, Dark grey

Page Header:
- Arial Bold 14pt, Black

*Sample GUI layout for web page*

You may wish to create your designs by hand.

Many IDEs, such as Visual Studio, have inbuilt designers for screen interaction. As these are very quick to develop screen designs, you could simply take a screenshot of a design and comment on it.

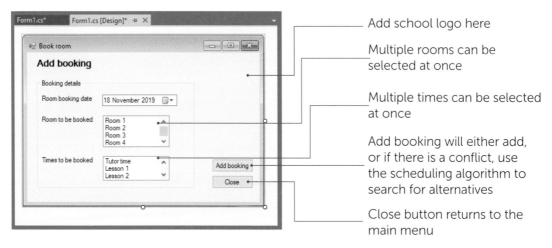

Add school logo here

Multiple rooms can be selected at once

Multiple times can be selected at once

Add booking will either add, or if there is a conflict, use the scheduling algorithm to search for alternatives

Close button returns to the main menu

When creating a design there is no need for object and file names to be changed. Produce these diagrams the fastest way that you can ready for implementation.

**WARNING** Whilst properties created by an IDE such as Form1 or button1 are no problem for a screen design, these will need to be changed in the implementation of the actual solution.

 Create designs for the user interface.

# Hardware selection

If your project makes use of standard hardware such as a Windows® PC, then you do not need to mention hardware selection or design.

Some projects will need custom hardware. For instance, this may be a specialist input device such as a barcode scanner. Other projects may make extensive use of hardware, for instance, if using an Arduino or Raspberry Pi to control components such as motors, buttons and LEDs.

In these cases, make a list of the hardware required and create a design of how it will be put together. This may be specification details about the hardware required or circuit diagrams of how it will be put together.

TASK If your project requires non-standard hardware then create a selection of designs for the hardware.

# Fully articulated designs

You need to show that you have a fully articulated design for your project. If you are using an iterative approach then it is likely that this will be built up over time.

It will depend on the project or investigation that you have chosen as to which of the above design techniques should be used. Some projects may require a deep level of design for a small number of techniques, whilst other projects may require designs for many of the above areas.

The purpose of the designs is that the third party (such as your teacher or moderator) can understand how the solution works overall. This requires both designs at an overall level and at a more specific level.

Only the key aspects of the solution or investigation need to be covered in order to be considered a fully articulated design.

> **TIP** It is important to focus on the design of key parts of the solution/investigation. Unimportant or trivial parts that require little thought do not need to be evidenced.

# Carrying out your design section

The design section should fit together in a coherent manner. It is often not the best approach to have separate sections for each aspect of the design such as UI design, algorithm design, SQL samples etc.

Instead, it is often better to work through key components of the design, working on the design of each one fully before going to the next.

For example, for a project that involved making a complicated school-wide calendar that had multiple users and scheduled events to avoid clashes, one component may be the scheduling of events. The design could consider covering the following for this component:

- Sketch the UI
- Discuss the algorithm(s) responsible for scheduling events and finding clashes
- Discuss any SQL queries required
- Discuss any key data structures and how the algorithms will manipulate these

Once this part of the solution had been designed, you could then move on to the next component. This method helps in giving a fully articulated design which is required for the top mark band of the Design section.

> **TIP** Remember that the tasks on the following to do list should only be carried out if they are relevant to your project. Many different design techniques may be used when discussing each component of the system you intend to build.

## To do list
Have you done the following?

- [ ] Written an overview of how the system works
- [ ] Given a written overview to introduce each diagram or table
- [ ] Created a structure/hierarchy chart
- [ ] If appropriate for your project, created a system flowchart
- [ ] If using Object-Oriented Programming (OOP), created a class diagram
- [ ] If appropriate, created a Data Flow Diagram (DFD)
- [ ] If using a database, created the database design
- [ ] If using a database, created the database queries
- [ ] If using a database, created an Entity-Relationship (E-R) diagram
- [ ] Created and shown key algorithms
- [ ] Identified key data structures used in the system
- [ ] If appropriate, shown file structures of the system
- [ ] Drawn HCI / screen designs
- [ ] If appropriate, selected and listed or designed any hardware requirements

# Chapter 5
## Technical solution

## Objectives

- Be able to demonstrate that the system meets the objectives of the solution/investigation
- Understand the importance of commenting code and self-documenting techniques
- Demonstrate technical skills of an appropriate level
- Demonstrate excellent coding styles

## The technical solution

The technical solution that you produce is worth more than half the marks for your project. As such, it is most likely that it will take up the majority of your project time.

Roughly 1/3 of the marks of your solution are for the completeness of solution, with the remainder being for the techniques and coding styles that you have used.

## Evidencing the technical solution

Full code listings of your technical solution should be given in your report. This should be placed in the Appendix section of your report and referred to from within the report.

Given the importance of your computer code towards your mark, remember the following advice, that code should:

- Contain useful comments that explain difficult algorithms/part of the code.
- The code should be self-documenting, meaning that it can, in general, be read without additional explanations. Using meaningful identifiers will help here.
- Use appropriate file names. When putting code into the report, include titled sections for each major part or file so that it is obvious what will be included.

## Source code

You will need to put the source code that you produce into the report. The code can be copied and pasted from an IDE quickly and efficiently. Copying and pasting will be better than taking screenshots. The text size can be increased or decreased in the word processor, and the file size of the report will remain small, which may make opening and editing faster.

If code is copied and pasted it will be clearer when printed. The moderator will also be able to zoom in if it is hard to read. This is not possible with a screenshot.

```
static float multiply(float num1, float num2)
{
    float result = num1 * num2;
    return result;
}
```

```
static float multiply(float num1, float num2)
{
    float result = num1 * num2;
    return result;
}
```

*Text may be clearer if it is copied and pasted (left) rather than a screenshot (right)*

There are times when a screenshot will work better, such as when showing feedback from the IDE during testing.

Copying and pasting source code has some drawbacks. It can become hard to follow if it goes over a page. For this reason, it is important to add titles to different files or sections of code.

Auto-formatting within a word processor may also be a problem, making your code look like it does not work or has not been indented correctly. If you decide to copy and paste code then be careful to ensure that it appears as it would in the IDE.

## Code contents page

Either within the report or at the front of the Appendix, you should make a contents page for the computer code. This will helps to identify key parts of the code and provides a pointer to complex areas along with page numbers.

| Code file/section | Details/purpose | Page(s) |
|---|---|---|
| Enemy Class | Inherits from the Main class | 70-75 |
| Move method | Uses the A* path finding algorithm | 72 |

*Example of part of a code contents page*

**TASK** Copy all your code listings into an Appendix in your report. Add titles to show which filenames the code has come from and also key parts of the code. Create a contents page to help your teacher and moderator find key parts of the code.

# Completeness of solution

You will get marks for the completeness of your solution compared to the objectives that you set out to achieve.

If some of your objectives were very hard and beyond A level standard, you will not be marked down for failing to achieve these. However, if your objectives were too easy and you meet them all, then you won't necessarily get full marks even if you do complete them all. For this reason, you should focus on having objectives that are hard enough to access technical skills from Group A.

You should aim to meet all the objectives of your system. Appropriate testing of your code will help in providing evidence that you have met the objectives.

It is a good idea to make a copy of your objectives in a table form. Create a column next to each objective which can refer to the evidence that shows that it was met including, where appropriate, a page number. The evidence may be from test results (in the next section of the report), video evidence, user feedback or code listings.

> **TIP**
> You can still get into the top mark band level if a few of your objectives aren't met. You need to consider whether your time is better spent fixing problems with your solution, or completing other parts of the report to a higher standard.

| Objectives | Achieved | Evidence |
|---|---|---|
| 4. Parents need to be informed of the appointments that they have just made. | ✓ | Testing p.63 |
| 1.1. Once they have confirmed the appointment a page will be displayed which contains<br>1.1.1. The appointment times<br>1.1.2. The names of the teachers<br>1.1.3. The subject for each teacher | ✓ | Screenshot p.65 |
| 4.2 A print button will be on the confirmation page. When clicked this will print all the appointment details given in objective 4.1 | ✓ | Video [1m32s] |

*An example showing evidence for a section of objectives being achieved*

> **TASK** Create evidence to show the completeness of the solution.

# Techniques used

You will be awarded a mark for the techniques that you have used in your programming. Be aware, the marks here are given for what you actually manage to successfully program, not what you planned in the Design section.

The code listings which you evidence will help to establish the use of techniques. You may wish to highlight specific areas of achievement by referencing a short video of your solution (or investigation) running.

Make sure that your code contains comments that highlight where techniques have been used – especially those that are in Group A of Table 1 in the mark scheme.

You should be aware that the mark you achieve will be based on:
- Use of technical skills
- How well the technical skills have been implemented
- Use of coding styles (see next section)
- How effective the solution is

To help demonstrate the effectiveness of the solution, you again may wish to reference a short video of it or provide feedback from an end-user(s) or supervisor.

Your Design section will be helpful in understanding the code that you have written. If, for example, you have used an algorithm or data structure that you explained thoroughly in the Design section, then you can refer back to this with a comment in the code.

> **TIP** You can make notes on your code listings to highlight the technical skills and techniques that you have used.

## Coding styles

The style of code which you use will make a difference to the mark you are awarded for techniques. This is something you need to consider right at the start of your coding, as it will be very difficult to change once you have built your solution.

Whilst the mark scheme classifies different coding styles into the categories of Excellent, Good and Basic, in order to achieve an Excellent coding style, you will need to also achieve the characteristics required for Good and Basic.

Your mark is evidenced through the overall quality of your code, not just one section that demonstrates good coding style.

> **TIP** You do not need to highlight features of good coding style as your teacher and moderator will be able to observe this from your code. You may, however, like to highlight key features of your modules and how they are organised, either using comments in the code or in the report.

# Chapter 5
## Technical solution

The following example shows a small section of code and how it can demonstrate many of the features of Basic, Good and Excellent coding styles.

| | |
|---|---|
| Use of constants (Good) Minimal use of global variables (Good) | Meaningful identifier (Basic) Modularisation of code (Good) |

Annotation used effectively where required (Good)

```
static void calculateArea()
{
    //calculates the area required for triangles that have a base of 5
    Console.Write("Base: ");
    String userBase = Console.ReadLine();
    Boolean numberEntered = false;
    const int testBase = 5;
    while (!numberEntered)
    {
        try
        {
            Console.Write(triangleArea((Double) testBase,
                            Convert.ToDouble(userBase)));
            numberEntered = true;
        }
        catch
        {
            Console.Write("A number must be entered. Base: ");
            userBase = Console.ReadLine();
        }
    }
}
```

Meaningful identifier (Basic) Good use of local variables (Good)

Managed casting of types (Good)

Good exception handling (Excellent)

Appropriate indentation (Good)

Subroutines with appropriate interfaces (Excellent) Loosely couple subroutines – code interacts with other parts through interface only (Excellent)

```
static Double triangleArea(Double theBase, Double height)
{
    //returns the area of a triangle
    return 0.5 * theBase * height;
}
```

Subroutines with common purpose grouped (Excellent) Cohesive modules - Subroutines do just one thing (Excellent)

```
static Double circleArea(Double radius)
{
    return PI * radius * radius;
}
```

Good coding style will also be demonstrated through:

- Creating self-documenting code – this is achieved by using good identifier names, well-organised code and annotation/comments. Each of these techniques will make the code possible to read and understand without any additional documentation
- Use of a consistent style throughout – there are different styles of indentation, variable naming and validation that can be carried out. It doesn't matter which you choose, but keep these consistent throughout your code
- Parameterised file paths – If you are reading or writing to files then you should not refer to a path such as 'C:\Users\TSmith' as this would only work on one computer. Instead, you could use relative pages such as '..\documents\May2010.pdf' or use environment variables such as '%HOMEPATH%\SchedulingSystem'
- Creating a well-designed user interface – to do this, consider how the design helps the user with labels and titles and a neat arrangement of objects

For outstanding code quality, your program will also need to use defensive programming techniques. This means that the program will continue to work even if unforeseen circumstances occur. Techniques and skills that will help in demonstrating defensive programming include:

- Making sure the program code is fully tested and all errors are fixed
- Using good exception handling
- Validating user input and handling invalid data in a predictable manner
- Making sure that the source code is readable

| TIP | You do not need to comment every line of code, but your comments should explain what key modules/functions/procedures do and any difficult to understand individual lines or sections of code. |
|---|---|

| TASK | During or at the end of each iteration, check your code quality for the following: <ul><li>Appropriate and meaningful identifier names (for modules and variables</li><li>Comments added to explain modules and difficult to understand code</li><li>Annotation or comments to refer to key algorithms, data structures or other designs that have been planned for in the Design section</li><li>Good coding features such as the use of modular code, use of local variables where possible, type conversion/casting, indentation of code, self-documenting code and consistent style</li><li>Excellent coding features such as exception handling, defensive programming, grouping related modules together, and modules that only interact through their interfaces (e.g. using arguments and return statements)</li></ul> |
|---|---|

# Chapter 5
## Technical solution

## To do list
Have you done the following?

☐ Completed your solution/investigation

☐ Copied all code listings to an Appendix

☐ Added appropriate titles/headings to the code

☐ Created a contents page for the code that allows easy location of different sections

☐ Made sure that the quality of the code uses expected coding styles

☐ Made sure that the reader is directed towards parts of the code that show more challenging technical skills

☐ Demonstrated the completeness of the solution compared to the objectives created in the Documented design section.

# Chapter 6
## Testing

## Objectives

- Produce evidence of thorough testing of the solution
- Cross-reference testing with the objectives
- Understand the types of evidence that can be used for the Testing section

## Introduction

It is important that the testing you carry out of your solution shows that your solution both works and is robust.

You may choose to undertake the testing as you develop the program, during or at the end of each iteration. Equally, testing can be undertaken once the program is completely finished.

Regardless of when you complete the tests, you should make sure to include evidence of testing in the Testing section of your report, or at least refer to other previous pages that have evidence of tests. There is no need to repeat tests that you have carried out earlier.

| TIP | Typically your testing will be done at the end once you have finished all coding, but there is no need to repeat previous tests if you have recorded them. |
|-----|---|

Any of the following may be used for evidence of testing:
- Formal test tables showing inputs and outputs
- Video evidence of the program working with different inputs/scenarios
- Screenshots with annotation of parts of the program working
- References to other sections that show testing during iterative development

# Chapter 6
Testing

# Sufficient testing

Be aware that the testing section of your report is only worth just over 10% of the total marks. Therefore, it should not be an overly arduous task.

In carrying out tests, it is essential that you focus on the core requirements of the solution. For instance, if you were building a game to teach tree traversal to A-level students, and the game automatically adapted to the ability of the student, then the key tests would focus around the core requirement that the game adapts to the student ability. If instead, the tests focused on the high-score table then it would be hard to award a high mark.

> **TIP** It is important to focus your tests on the core requirements.

When testing you should carefully select representative samples of tests and test data which will demonstrate key parts of the program working.

# Iterative testing

Testing iteratively can be done at any time during an iteration and does not always have to be after you have written all of the code.

Remember that when you compile and run the program you are already carrying out testing. At this stage, you should record what has been tested and check appropriate test cases.

Failed tests show solid development strategy and understanding. No one writes a perfect piece of complex software correctly at the first try. The exam board knows that there will be errors and issues encountered along the way.

> **TIP** Repeating lots of tests for minor objectives in your program will add to your workload, but gain few if any additional marks.

Note that you do not need to show any evidence of iterative testing. However, if you have provided evidence of testing your program as it has been developed then these tests do not need to be repeated.

## Strong iterative testing features

Strong iterative testing will have the following features:
- Summarise the tests which worked using a range of suitable evidence
- Demonstrate a few of the tests which have passed, focusing on the more interesting ones or the ones that show the system has met a core objective
- Discuss the reason why non-trivial tests failed, showing a clear line of thought to a solution
- Prove the error has been fixed

# Post-development testing

Once the solution or investigation is completed it must be fully tested. This testing looks at the system as a whole.

Remember that most of the program such as modules, classes and algorithms may already have been tested as part of the iterative testing. The focus of post-development testing is to show that everything works together as one robust unit.

The tests you undertake should be similar to how a user may use the system. Whilst you will have an intimate experience of how your system was built, you need to put yourself in the shoes of a user for the purposes of post-development testing.

The aim of the testing is to show that the system is robust and that the requirements/objectives of the solution have been met. An easy way to achieve this is to copy the objectives from the Design section and make suitable tests that show each one has been met.

## Strong post-development testing features

Strong post-development testing will have the following features:

- Avoid repeating any of the iterative tests already carried out
- Focus on the system as a whole, and not individual parts (unless they are core requirements and have not previously been tested)
- Mimic real-life user interactions
- Directly link to the original requirements in the objectives in the Design section

# Evidencing testing

## Test tables

Tables can be a very useful way of recording test evidence. These can easily be based on objectives and are a methodical way of showing both the robustness and completeness of the solution. Be aware, though, that they may be time-consuming to create and video evidence may be faster.

> TIP | You do not need to show that tests have failed in your final testing. If a test does fail, then you will need to fix it and show that it has passed the re-test.

# Chapter 6
## Testing

| Objective | Test # | Input | Expected output | Actual output / screenshot / evidence | Pass/Fail | Comments |
|---|---|---|---|---|---|---|
| 3.1 – The quiz correctly asks differentiation questions of the type $d/dx\ (x^3) = 3x^2$ | 1 | 1 | 3 | 3 | Pass | |
| | 2 | 2 | 4 | 4 | Pass | |
| | 3 | -5 | -75 | Error | Fail | See p.59 for fix to this |
| | 3 | -5 | -75 | -75 | Pass | |
| | 4 | 10 | 300 | 300 | Pass | |

*Example of a section of testing using test tables*

Comments can be added to tests. There is no need to write obvious comments such as "It didn't work". Instead, add comments where they show understanding. For instance, "It appears that there is a logic error that occurs here when the function is called with large values." shows that an idea has already been considered for what may be causing the error.

## Video

Video is a very powerful evidence tool, and using it means that you can evidence that your solution works and is robust very quickly.

If a picture can tell 1,000 words, video can convey many more. Video can save you time taking multiple screenshots, each of which would need pasting, cropping and possibly editing.

Video is perfect for showing movement in games or transitions through a complex system. It can also record sound. Most modern smartphones record video and this is a good option to consider for physical projects.

Remember that videos will need editing. The software to record and capture video is generally free, but you need to be confident in using it.

Video length is something to be careful of. The video needs to be long enough to demonstrate that the system is fully working, but avoid endless trivial tests or making your teacher and moderator sit through an unnecessarily long video. Five to ten minutes is a typical video length to be sufficient to show the program fully working, the robustness of the solution and that the requirements of the objectives have been achieved. Of course, your video can be longer if your solution requires it.

Take care to plan the tests that you will need to demonstrate before recording so that your video is more concise and doesn't miss any important tests.

Be aware that if you provide video evidence you still need to complete test tables, but these will refer to the specific time of the test evidence in the video.

> **TIP** If you use video as evidence, see chapter 8 for more information about how AQA expects them to be submitted.

| Benefits | Drawbacks |
|---|---|
| • Shows transition and movement<br>• Very suited to games<br>• Can save a lot of time over screenshot evidence<br>• Screen recording software can be free | • Can generate large files<br>• Harder to reference<br>• Must timestamp every reference<br>• Not 'in the document' so must be clear where you are using video as evidence |

## Screenshots

Screenshots are the easiest method of evidence recording. They can be created without additional software and are good for recording evidence of parts of a program working.

There are drawbacks to screenshots. The most overlooked one is that your documentation file size will increase significantly. This can make it slow to open and edit the report.

Screenshots may also need cropping and create problems with text wrapping in the word processor that is used.

Visibility of screenshots is key. Very often marks are lost as the screenshot's resolution is too low, or the size too small. This makes it unreadable. Unreadable screenshots cannot be given any marks.

*Examples of screenshots where the text is too small to read*

> **WARNING** Make sure that any screenshots allow the moderator to read them to avoid losing marks.

| Benefits | Drawbacks |
|---|---|
| • Quick to make<br>• Do not require special software<br>• Good at capturing development over time | • Usually needs cropping<br>• Word wrapping and formatting<br>• Potential for poor resolution<br>• Shrinking screenshots can leave them unreadable<br>• Taking too many screenshots will slow you down<br>• Makes document file size large |

## Photos

Taking photos with a smartphone or a digital camera can also be an option. Photos may be more appropriate if you are working with physical computing solutions. For example, a photograph of a robot navigating a maze would be able to show distinct abilities far better than a screenshot of the computer code.

Photos will need to be transferred and cropped for the report. They share similar benefits and drawbacks with screenshots.

Note that for the majority of projects, photos are unlikely to be needed as screenshots are sufficient to show a program running on a display. However, for physical projects, or to show an end-user interacting with the product, photos may be the best form of evidence.

| Benefits | Drawbacks |
|---|---|
| • Easy to take<br>• Do not require special software<br>• Can get good quality from modern smartphones<br>• Good at capturing development over time<br>• Generally easy to transfer to PC | • Usually need cropping/editing<br>• File sizes from a modern smartphone tend to be large<br>• Word wrapping and formatting<br>• Shrinking photos of screens can leave text unreadable<br>• Makes document file size large |

TASK

Complete the testing of your system by (one or more of):
- post-development test tables
- referring back to iterative tests carried out earlier in the project
- video
- screenshots or photos

## To do list
Have you done the following?

☐ Shown evidence of thorough testing of your solution/investigation

☐ Shown evidence that all the core requirements of the solution/investigation have been achieved

☐ Selected representative samples of testing

☐ Demonstrated that the solution is robust or the investigation is thorough

☐ If appropriate, referred to iterative tests carried out previously in the report

☐ If appropriate, made a video of tests and referenced how to access it in the testing section (see Chapter 8 for how to submit video)

☐ If appropriate, take screenshots of testing

☐ If appropriate, created test tables of your testing

# Chapter 7
## Evaluation

<hr>

## Objectives

- Provide evidence of how well each of the requirements is met

- Be able to discuss detailed improvements

- Obtain independent feedback

- Evaluate the independent feedback

## Effective evaluation

If you have numbered your objectives and requirements, then this will make the Evaluation section a lot easier to write. It will also keep it clear and easy to follow.

Avoid the temptation of copying and pasting a lot of screenshots or code into your evaluation. If you have tested it already, refer back to it. This will save you time and reduce the amount of work to be done.

The evaluation must be critical. Being honest and open will give you more to write about. Errors and bugs are fine to discuss and will help in considering the limitations of the solution/ investigation and further development.

## Evaluating the solution as a whole

You should first evaluate the solution as a whole. Consider how well it solves the overall problem that your end-user(s) or stakeholders were experiencing or the problem that you were investigating if you are carrying out an investigation.

Remember that this evaluation should be critical. Even if it meets all the requirements, make sure you have given both good features of the solution and ways it could be improved. Bringing in the opinions and experiences of the solution from your end-user(s), stakeholders or supervisor is also useful at this point.

# Evaluating how well the requirements are met

In order to evaluate how well your solution/investigation has met the requirements in your objectives, you need to go through and evaluate each of them. When doing this you should give:

- Your own critical evaluation – what are the positives or negatives of the solution/investigation for each objective?
- Independent feedback – what does your end-user(s)/supervisor or another third party think of how well you have met each objective?
- What is your evaluation of their feedback?
- How could the system/investigation be improved?

You may wish to complete this as a table that maps against each of your objectives, or as written prose related to each of the objectives.

| **TIP** | Try to include critical comments that show your depth of understanding about how you have implemented your solution/investigation. Trivial comments such as "it's slow" are not as useful as explaining the reason for the problem and how it could be improved. |
|---|---|

The following examples are made with reference to the following example objectives:

5. Admin staff need to be able to look up appointments for a parent. This may be carried out on behalf of a teacher request or parent contacting the school.
   5.1. Admin staff will be able to put a student's name into a search box
   5.2. This will then find all the appointments that their parents have made (same details as 4.1)
   5.3. Admin staff can carry out the following appointment functions:
      5.3.1. Add new appointments
      5.3.2. Edit existing appointments
      5.3.3. Delete appointments
   5.4. When the admin staff click the "Confirm changes" button, the new appointments are sent in a confirmation email to the parent

## Your evaluation

The evaluation that you make needs to be specific and critical of your solution/investigation. It should balance both positive and negative comments and base these on both objective and subjective reasoning. Where possible, consider evaluations that have a Computer Science background to them.

# Chapter 7
## Evaluation

You should refer back to your objectives, or copy and paste them to this section so that they can be commented on directly.

"I feel that objective 5.1 has been met very well. The solution allows the first or last name of the student to be entered into the search box and if more than one student matches this name then a list of potential students to choose is given. This makes it very easy to use without the end-user having to consider which way to enter the data. This would also reduce the need for training or help within the system. By using SQL queries and MySQL, the queries execute incredibly fast, meaning that the user doesn't need to wait for the results. This goes beyond what was expected to meet the objective.

Given this is an online system, the search box could be further improved to match how search engines like Google® work. For instance, as the name is being entered, a drop-down list of suggested searches could be given. This would make it faster to enter names. It would also make it easier to find names that are harder to spell. Recent searches could also be given. This would involve a new table in the database that would store the search criteria, user ID and date/time that it was made.

At the moment, when no student is found, the system is robust in that it says 'no student found'. However, this isn't very helpful. It would be better if it looked for similar names or misspellings. This may be hard to program or inefficient – so an easy algorithm to solve this may be to look at the first two letters and then give a list of potential students that way. A simple SQL query with wildcard characters could achieve this."

*An example of part of an effective critical evaluation of one objective*

The above example has the following features of a good evaluation:
- It mentions the objective(s) it is applying to
- It is specific about why the current solution meets the objective
- It gives specific reasons why the solution has met this well
- It shows the limitations of the current solution
- It makes useful suggestions as to how the solution could be improved
- Explanations of achievements and improvements are grounded in Computer Science reasoning

> **TIP** Not every objective needs an evaluation of this depth. The depth required will depend on how trivial the objective is and how many you have to complete. If you have many objectives then choose a few core ones to evaluate in detail.

Copy all the objectives/requirements from your Design section. Write a critical evaluation for each one.

# Independent feedback

Your evaluation needs to incorporate independent feedback from a third party. Ideally, this should be one or more of the end-users for your solution or the supervisor of your investigation.

Comments from your third party such as "It's good" or "it works well" are not specific enough to be useful. You need to encourage them to give details of why it is good, why it works well for them and what improvements could be made. You may also wish to comment on observations that you make of them using the system.

> "One of the admin staff tried to add (5.3.1), edit (5.3.2) and delete (5.3.1) appointments. These were all the features of objective 5.3 and they used a test email account and student to test 5.4.
>
> They stated that they found it really easy to carry out all these actions and they particularly liked the way that an email was automatically sent to the parent (5.4). However, the system only allows one parent to be sent an email. They suggested that it would be better if it allowed two email addresses to be entered. They also commented that very often they don't know the email address to send to, so having an option to not send an email would be useful."

*An example of part of an evaluation showing independent feedback*

The above example has the following features of a good evaluation:
- It mentions the objective(s) it is applying to
- The feedback is useful and realistic
- The feedback gives specific reasons why the system has performed/not performed well
- Suggestions are given on how the system could be improved

Go through each of your objectives/requirements with your end-user(s)/supervisor/third party to see how well they think you have met them. Incorporate their feedback into your evaluation.

# Evaluation of independent feedback

To achieve the highest marks for the evaluation, you need to evaluate and discuss the feedback that you have been given.

Comments such as "I agree" or "this would be too hard" are not specific enough as they neither evaluate or give a discussion as to why this is the case.

> "The comments regarding preventing the sending of emails would be easy to implement. A checkbox could be ticked if an email is to be sent and a second textbox could be added. If the checkbox is unticked then the email textboxes could be disabled to prevent entering an email address. It would be easy to change the program code for this as the sendEmail(address) function could just be called for each email address.
>
> However, the comment suggested that they often don't know the email address. The system would be even better if it synchronised the email addresses with those in the school's Management Information System (MIS). It could then allow email addresses to be selected from a list of possible choices (or entered by hand). This would be a further improvement to the suggestions, however, it would require extensive processing to get the information from the MIS and process it."

*An example of evaluation and discussion of independent feedback*

The above example has the following features of a good evaluation:
- Evaluative comments have been given regarding the feedback
- A discussion has been given as to how the interface could be changed
- Suggestions as to how this could be implemented are given
- Further discussion is given of a better way to solve the problem in the feedback with a suitable evaluation of the strengths and weaknesses of the idea

 TASK | Write evaluative comments on the statements that your third party has given.

## To do list
Have you done the following?

☐ Evaluated how well each of the requirements/objectives have been met

☐ Given reasons, including technical as to why parts of the solution have been programmed well or not so well

☐ Identified areas of the solution that could be improved

☐ Obtained independent feedback that is useful and realistic

☐ Evaluated and discussed the independent feedback in a meaningful way

# Chapter 8
## Final checks

## Objectives

- Review your project and report against the mark scheme
- Ensure the report is laid out well
- Check for referencing and third party material
- Ensure that the report has been proof-read
- Understand how to submit your report and any video evidence

## Checking evidence in the report

> **TIP**
> The following suggestions show ideas for how you can check you have met all the criteria on the mark scheme. Whilst you don't have to do these, you may find it useful for making sure that you have covered everything needed in the report. Choose the method that works best for you.

### Compare against checklists

First, check that you have carried out all the tasks in this book. Then go through each of the 'To do' lists and make sure you have carried out each item. Check off each one as a record of completion. The tasks have been closely aligned with what is needed in the mark scheme.

### Compare against the mark scheme

Now is the time to take a clean copy of the mark scheme and check that you have covered all areas given in it.

> **TIP**
> Your teacher may have created a version of the mark scheme for you to use. Check you understand what is required at each section before starting this process.

Now, simply use a highlighter with a printed copy of the mark scheme. Read each section and highlight any parts that you can find good evidence for. At the end of this process, any areas that are not highlighted need more evidence.

If you think that you need to do some extra work in any section, mark it down for improvement. Your teacher can then give you some generic feedback as to whether you could develop any sections you have highlighted. For instance, they may say that your testing needs to be developed in order to satisfy the criteria of the top mark band level, however, they cannot tell you exactly what to do to improve.

Always consider the time needed to add more evidence against the marks which will be gained. Spending ten hours to gain a couple of marks on some minor features of the solution will not be as effective as spending three hours completing the Testing section to take it from Level 2 to Level 4 on the mark scheme.

| TASK | Compare your report against the criteria given in the mark scheme. |
|---|---|

# Documentation and evidence

Your documentation is essential for success in the project and proving your system works. Information should be presented in a logically structured manner.

It is worth spending some time reviewing the layout. The following checks should be carried out on your documentation:

- Each page has a suitable header and footer containing:
  - Candidate name
  - Candidate number
  - Centre name
  - Centre number
  - Project title
  - Page number

- The table of contents has been updated
- Each section has a clear heading and relates to part of the mark scheme
- Sub-headings are used effectively
- Screenshots are readable and clear
- References to evidence are accurate
- Wording is clear and concise
- Referencing is complete and accurate

# Chapter 8
**Final checks**

# Proof-reading and referencing

## Proof-reading

A **spellchecker** is usually an in-built component of the word processing package that has been used. Make sure you use it to help find any errors. Submitting work with poor spelling and grammar gives a bad impression.

Remember that spellcheckers will not catch all errors so be sure to leave time to read your work at least once from beginning to end. Confusing wording or inaccurate use of terminology can lose you marks if they cause the moderator to misunderstand what is being said.

> TASK    Proof-read and spellcheck your report.

## Referencing

Not referencing sources that you have used is considered cheating. If you are found to have used sources, and not referenced them, then you may:

- receive zero marks for your work
- be stopped from taking your A Level

Markers and moderators must be able to see the following:

- What has been copied or come from another source
- That the source has been acknowledged
- Where/how you have developed the source material into your own project or words

Your school or the exam board may use plagiarism checkers. These are sophisticated in flagging up areas of reports or projects that have been copied.

> TASK    Make sure you have included a references section and all sources have been correctly referenced.

# Submitting video evidence

It is perfectly acceptable to submit video evidence for your project. It is most likely that this will be used for evidence of testing.

No electronic work may be submitted to the exam board, however, the moderator will be able to view evidence that is publicly accessible. It is suggested that YouTube or Google Drive are used for this as both services are reliable. You may have a personal account to upload evidence, or a department or school account may be used.

In order to use video evidence:

- Check with your teacher how they want you to submit the video. Some teachers may have a school/college YouTube account, some may ask you to use a personal account, whilst others may use a shared Google Drive or similar file-sharing site
- Make sure the video has been uploaded
- Test that it plays correctly
- Make sure that the settings allow the general public to access the video
- Add the links to the videos into your report – make sure that the full URL is printed, not hyperlinked with an underline
- If uploading the video to a file-sharing site (such as Google Drive) make sure that it is in MP4 format and test it on at least two different devices to see that it plays correctly

| TIP | To make it easier for your teacher and moderator to check your video evidence, provide a full list/table of all video titles and their URLs as an Appendix. Your teacher may also make their own list of videos used by each student in the class. |
|---|---|

When giving the URL to your video, remember the following:

- Remove the hyperlink formatting in the document as it will be printed
- Use an easily readable font such as Courier New
- Check that letters such as 1, i, I, l and L are easy to differentiate
- Ask someone else to check that they can enter the URL without difficulty

| TASK | Make a list of any video URLs and titles which you have made as evidence. |
|---|---|

## Submitting your report

Your report must be submitted in paper form.

When submitting your work you must include:

- The paper report
- A signed Candidate Record Form (CRF)
- If you are providing video evidence, then the links (URLs) of the videos

The report should be hole punched in the top left corner with a treasury tag through all the pages to hold it together.

| WARNING | Do not put your report in a folder or ring binder. |
|---|---|

# Chapter 8
## Final checks

Finally, check that each page number has printed and is in your report. If any evidence is missing then you may well lose marks. Be aware of any deadlines that your teacher has given and make sure you submit your work well before the deadline.

## Deadline for submitting your report

Deadline for printing report: _____

Deadline for handing in report: _____

## To do list
### Have you done the following?

☐ Checked your report against the To do lists in this book

☐ Checked your report against the mark scheme

☐ Made sure that key documentation and evidence is present

☐ Proof-read your work

☐ Checked that any copied materials have been correctly referenced

☐ Uploaded videos

☐ Created a list of all video evidence

☐ Completed a Candidate Record Form (CRF)

☐ Printed the report and attached it to the CRF with a treasury tag

☐ Handed in the report

# Index

# Appendix
## Useful shortcuts and key combinations

### Editing shortcut key combinations

| | |
|---|---|
| **Ctrl + A** | Select all |
| **Ctrl + B** | Apply or remove bold formatting |
| **Ctrl + C** | Copy |
| **Ctrl + Shift + C** | Copy formatting |
| **Ctrl + F** | Find |
| **Ctrl + I** | Apply or remove italic formatting |
| **Ctrl + P** | Print |
| **Ctrl + S** | Save |
| **Ctrl + V** | Paste |
| **Ctrl + Shift + V** | Paste formatting |
| **Ctrl + X** | Cut |
| **Ctrl + Y** | Redo or repeat last action |
| **Ctrl + Z** | Undo an action |
| **Shift + F3** | Toggle case |
| **Alt + =** | Insert equation |
| **Shift + Enter** | Create a soft line break |
| **Ctrl + Enter** | Insert a page break |
| **Ctrl + [** | Decrease font size |
| **Ctrl + ]** | Increase font size |

### Navigation shortcuts

| | |
|---|---|
| **Ctrl + Home** | Go to beginning of document |
| **Ctrl + End** | Go to end of document |
| **Shift + F5** | Go to last place text was edited |